Oxford Stage Company & Dumbfounded Theatre
present

T0262455

PROFESSOR BERNHARDI
A COMEDY

By **Arthur Schnitzler**
In a new version by **Samuel Adamson**

Directed by **Mark Rosenblatt**
Design by **Jon Bausor**
Lighting by **Tim Mascall**
Sound by **Adrienne Quartly**

First performance of this production as part of **The Last Waltz Season**
on 29 March 2005 at the Arcola Theatre, London.

The Last Waltz Season also features *Musik* by Frank Wedekind, translated
and adapted by Neil Fleming, and *Rose Bernd* by Gerhart Hauptmann, in
a new version by Dennis Kelly.

GOETHE-INSTITUT LONDON

arcola theatre

wellcometrust

austrian cultural forum[lon]

Oxford Stage Company is supported by

ARTS COUNCIL ENGLAND

Oxford Stage Company and Dumbfounded Theatre present

PROFESSOR BERNHARDI
A COMEDY
by **Arthur Schnitzler**

Cast

At the Elisabeth Institute, a private teaching hospital, Vienna, c.1900:

Mr Hochroitzpointner,   Roger Evans
a student of medicine

Nurse Ludmilla   Mariah Gale

Dr Oskar Bernhardi,   Tom Godwin
Professor Bernhardi's son and assistant

Dr Kurt Pflugfelder,   Bertie Carvel
first assistant to Professor Bernhardi

Professor Bernhardi,   Christopher Godwin
Director of the Institute

Professor Ebenwald,   Dale Rapley
Vice-Director of the Institute

Professor Tugendvetter,   John Dougall
Professor of Dermatology and Syphilis

Dr Adler,   John Lloyd Fillingham
Lecturer in Pathological Anatomy

Professor Cyprian,   Fred Pearson
Professor of Neuropathy

Professor Filitz,   Bertie Carvel
Professor of Gynaecology

Dr Löwenstein,   John Dougall
Lecturer in Paediatrics

Dr Schreimann,   Deka Walmsley
Lecturer in Throat Disease

Professor Pflugfelder,   John Stahl
Professor of Optometry and Kurt's father

Dr Wenger,   Jake Harders
assistant to Professor Tugendvetter

From the Church of St Florian:

Father Franz Reder   Jake Harders

At the Ministry of Education and Cultural Affairs:

His Excellency Dr Flint   John Stahl
Privy Counsellor Winkler   Deka Walmsley

A Secretary   Caroline Hayes

Representing Bernhardi:

Dr Goldenthal,   Deka Walmsley
Bernhardi's Defence Counsel

At Bernhardi's Home:

Housekeeper   Caroline Hayes

All other parts played by members of the company.

The cast of *Professor Bernhardi* is drawn from an ensemble of actors which also includes: Lucy Briers, Cydney Folan and Yvonne Gidden.

Creative Team

Adaptor	Samuel Adamson
Director	Mark Rosenblatt
Designer	Jon Bausor
Lighting Designer	Tim Mascall
Sound Designer	Adrienne Quartly
Season Lighting Designers	Tim Mascall & Neil Sloan
Literal Translator	Nadja Sumichrast
Costume Supervisor	Sallyann Dicksee
Assistant Director	Lydia Ziemke
Assistant Designers	Anna Jones
	Tom Rogers
Production Manager	Chris Umney
Stage Managers	Laura Farrell
	Nicholas Green
Assistant Stage Managers	Sarah Grange
	Ciara Fanning
Production Electrician	Jenny Abbott
Production Photographer	Alessandro Evangelista
Graphic Design	Pansy Aung & Winnie
Wong	
Season Producers	Mark Rosenblatt
	Neil Laidlaw

Production Acknowledgements

Petra Tauscher, Conrad Lynch, Sibylle Wunderlich, Gemma Hancock, Anne McNulty, Anneliese Davidsen, The Young Vic, Linzie Hunter at Mountview Academy, Paul Anderson at Sparks Theatrical Hire, Charlotte Windmill at Oxford Shakespeare Company, Simon Cranidge at the National Theatre, Mary Green, James Granville, Jonathan Evans, Archivist at The Royal London Hospital, the staff of the British Library, the London Library and the Goethe Institute.

Special thanks to

Sir Tom Stoppard, Peter Skrine, David Lan, Patricia Benecke, Claire Frewin, The Wellcome Trust, Austrian Cultural Forum, Mercers' Charitable Foundation and the Academy of Young Jewish Artists.

A rehearsed reading of this version of *Professor Bernhardi* was performed in conjunction with the Caird Company as part of its New Directions Season at the Theatre Royal Haymarket. We would like to thank the Caird Company for their support in the development of this text.

A note on this version

Professor Bernhardi (1912) is rarely translated into English. The only readily available English version for most of the twentieth century, from the 1936 London production (directed by Schnitzler's son, Heinrich), now seems a curiously emasculated affair. The play demands cutting, as long as you don't cut the good stuff. With its conspicuous veil over some of the characters' anti-Semitism and its prudish attitude towards Philomena Beier's abortion, it tells us much more about 1936 than it does about 1912 (or 1900, when the play is set). But that's the trouble with versions, adaptations and translations, and some good stuff is missing from this new text, though for tiresome 2005 reasons: today few people are fond of long plays and few professional companies can afford to employ 20 or more actors. Hence Feuermann, a young Jewish GP who inadvertently kills one of his patients and fruitlessly seeks the support of Bernhardi, Filitz and Flint, has been omitted here (though as an off-stage character he remains part of the dramatic texture). His lengthy sub-plot, though darkly comic, is a diversion, largely reported second-hand, with little bearing on the Bernhardi story. Kulka, a liberal journalist who offers to publicise Bernhardi's case, has also been excised. In Act Four, I've implemented the one cut made in 1936 that I happen to agree with: by removing most of the dialogue after the Priest's exit, helpful dramatic emphasis is placed on his scene with Bernhardi. Should directors wish to reinstate this material, it is provided (*sans* Kulka) in the appendix. For the benefit of English-speaking actors and audiences, there are minor tucks and clarifications throughout this text. These and the above changes should be attributed to me and not to my colleague Nadja Sumichrast, who provided the fastidious literal translation from which I made my version. My thanks to her and Mark Rosenblatt.

Samuel Adamson
London, March 2005

Professor Bernhardi

Last year I spent a little too much time in the British Library. My mission was to find 3 rarely (if ever) seen plays by great German writers from around the turn of the 20th century. I'm a big fan of the equivalent period of British theatre (Bernard Shaw, Granville Barker, Galsworthy, DH Lawrence) and, having German grandparents, I was curious to know what German theatre was up to before Brecht burst on to the scene and eclipsed virtually everybody. I found a wealth of plays, some awful, some ok, and a handful of gems.

Sometimes you read a play and know you have to direct it, no matter what. Coming from a German-Jewish background, I have an unfortunate fascination with plays that deal with the roots of anti-Semitism. And *Professor Bernhardi* is the best I've read. It is about gentlemen of great intelligence and culture for whom the Holocaust would have been a lunatic's sick joke. And yet, amidst the heel-clicking, top hats, sophistication and innovation, the seeds are well and truly sown for a bleak and terrifying future.

Last November the (sadly now defunct) Caird Company allowed me to try the play out in a reading at the Haymarket Theatre. In front of a small lunchtime crowd, this play of ideas became a comedy of human failings. Its humour, less evident in older, dustier translations, has been released brilliantly by our adaptor, Sam Adamson, who has an uncanny gift for evoking a period or capturing a character with the lightest, deftest turn of phrase.

Professor Bernhardi has not been seen in London since 1936. I should imagine its neglect owes a great deal to the size of the cast. I am very fortunate to be directing *Professor Bernhardi* as part of a repertory season whose greatest asset is its ensemble of actors. Many of the supporting roles in *Bernhardi* are played by leading actors in the other two shows. Such strength and depth has made *Professor Bernhardi* attemptable. I hope you think it worth the wait.

Mark Rosenblatt, 2005
Artistic Director
Dumbfounded Theatre

Cast in alphabetical order

BERTIE CARVEL Dr Kurt Pflugfelder / Professor Filitz
Training: RADA
Theatre: Credits include the title role in *Macbeth* (en masse for Union Theatre); *Victory?* (Donmar Theatre); and *Revelations* (Hampstead Theatre).
TV and Film: Credits include *The Genius of Beethoven* (BBC); *Bombshell* (Shed Productions for ITV); *Agatha Christie: A Life in Pictures* (Wall to Wall for BBC); *The Lost World of Mitchell and Kenyon* (BBC); *Suits and Swipes* (New York Film Academy) and *Hawking* (BBC).
Radio: Bertie has also recorded over 30 radio plays for the BBC, including *Trilby*, *Diary of a Nobody*, *The Odyssey*, *The Pallisers*, *Kamikaze*, *Portugal*, *D Day,* and *The Entertainer.*

JOHN DOUGALL Professor Tugendvetter / Dr Löwenstein
Training: Royal Scottish Academy of Music and Drama.
Theatre: Work for the Royal Shakespeare Company includes: *Hamlet, Love in a Wood, Macbeth* (Stratford / London / Japan / US), *Measure for Measure, The Two Gentlemen of Verona, The Merchant of Venice, The Cherry Orchard, Faust, The Devil is an Ass, Peter Pan, The Winter's Tale, The Crucible* (UK / Poland). Work for the English Shakespeare Company includes: *The Henrys, The War of the Roses, Richard II, Richard III, The Winter's Tale, Coriolanus,* and *Romeo and Juliet* (Old Vic, West End, national and international tours). Theatre credits in London include: *The Shadow of a Gunman, John Bull's Other Island* (Tricycle), *Measure for Measure* (Globe); *Americans, The Cherry Orchard* (Oxford Stage Company); *Another Country* (Queen's Theatre); *The Cherry Orchard* (Aldwych); *St Joan* (Strand); *Dr Faustus* (Greenwich Theatre); and *Twelfth Night, Macbeth* and *King Lear* (St George's Theatre). Other theatre includes: *Present Laughter* (Theatre Royal Bath / tour); *Arcadia* (Northampton / Salisbury); *Hay Fever* (Oxford Stage Company); *Romeo and Juliet* (Nottingham); *Of Mice and Men* (Birmingham); *Tess of the D'Urbervilles* (Edinburgh Festival); *The Comedy of Errors, Translations, Peter Pan* (Lyric, Belfast); *Lysistrata, Treasure Island* (Worcester); and *The Lass wi' the Muckle Mou* (Pitlochry).
TV: Credits include *The Houseman's Tale, Dunrulin', As Time Goes By, Taggart, The Bill, The Negotiator, Monarch of the Glen, Macbeth, Randall and Hopkirk (Deceased), He Knew He Was Right* and *Measure for Measure.*

ROGER EVANS Mr Hochroitzpointner
Theatre: Credits include *Woyzeck* (The Gate); *How Love is Spelt* (Bush Theatre); *The King Stag* (Young Vic Theatre); *Art and Guff* (Soho Theatre/ Sgript Cymru); *Everything Must Go* (Sherman Theatre); *Gas Station Angel* (Royal Court International tour); and *Scum &*

Civility and *The Man Who Never Yet Saw Woman's Nakedness* (Royal Court International Festival).
TV: *Casualty, Doctors, The Bill, Murphy's Law, Absolute Power, Nuts and Bolts, The Bench, Bradford In My Dreams, Sleeping With The TV On, A Mind to Kill, Rhinoceros, Crime Traveller,* and *Wonderful You*.
Film: *All or Nothing, Human Traffic,* and *Suckerfish*.

JOHN LLOYD FILLINGHAM Dr Adler
Training: Welsh College of Music and Drama.
Theatre: Credits include *Abigail's Party* (The Duke's, Lancaster); *Titus Andronicus, Measure for Measure, A Midsummer Night's Dream* and *The Taming of the Shrew* (all for the RSC); *The Birthday Party* (Crucible Theatre, Sheffield); *In Celebration* (Chichester Festival Theatre); *The Contractor* and *Making Noise Quietly* (Oxford Stage Company and West End); *Sleeping Around* (Paines Plough); *The Tempest, The Glass Menagerie, The Rise and Fall of Little Voice* (including national tour), *A Christmas Carol* (Bristol Old Vic); *The Glory of the Garden* (Duke of York's, London); *Road* and *The Doctor's Dilemma* (Royal Exchange, Manchester); *The Importance of Being Earnest, Spring and Port Wine* and *Waiting for Godot* (Octagon Theatre, Bolton); *The Comedy of Errors* and *The Tempest* (Nottingham Playhouse and international tour); *The Atheist's Tragedy* (Birmingham Repertory Theatre); *Amadeus* (Gateway, Chester); and *I Do* (National Theatre Studio).
TV: Credits include *Foyle's War, Casualty, Walter, My Secret Life, The Last Romantics, The Vice, A + E, Coronation Street, Cold Feet, September Song, Children's Ward, The Royal, Crocodile Shoes, The Bill, Spatz,* and *B & B.*
Radio: *The Ghost of Federico Garcia Lorca, Henry IV Parts I and II* and *School for Scandal* for BBC Radio 3; and *Healthy Pursuits, Cozzy's Last Stand, Letters of Introduction, Looking for Alice, Gabriella and The Gargoyles, Lost Empires, A Stone's Throw from the Sea, Stolen Kisses,* and *Pino Pelosi* for BBC Radio 4.

CHRISTOPHER GODWIN Professor Bernhardi
Theatre: Credits include *Home* (Oxford Stage Company). For the RSC: Gremio in *The Taming of the Shrew* and *The Tamer Tamed*, Belarius in *Cymbeline*, Coupler in *The Relapse*, Everill in *The Devil is an Ass* and Captain in *Woyzeck*. For the Open Air Theatre, Regent's Park: The King in *Henry IV Part 1*, Quince in *A Midsummer Night's Dream*, Capulet in *Romeo and Juliet*, Jacques in *As You Like It*, Don Armado in *Love's Labour's Lost* and Malvolio in *Twelfth Night*. Other London theatre includes *The Woman in Black* (Fortune); *What a Performance* (Queen's); *Noises Off* (Savoy); *Ten Times Table* (Gielgud); *Hay Fever* (Albery); *School for Scandal* (Haymarket); *The Guv'nor* (one-man show at the Young Vic); *All Things Considered* (Scarborough and Hampstead). Scarborough premières of *Time and Time Again, Absurd*

Person Singular, The Norman Conquests, Confusions and *Absent Friends.* Other regional theatre includes seasons at Canterbury, Cardiff, Dundee, Bolton, York, and Chichester.

TV: Credits include *Crisis Command, Murder in Mind, Strange, Casualty, Manchild, Innocents, Prince Among Men, Lovejoy, The Bill, Prince Caspian and the Voyage of the Dawn Treader, Nice Work, My Family and Other Animals, William Tell, Return to Treasure Island, Astronauts, Holding the Fort* and *Don't Be Silly.*

Film: Credits include *Blackball, The Avengers, Jinnah, A Handful of Dust, Bullshot, Porridge* and *Charlie Muffin.*

Radio: Numerous broadcasts, including the current series of *Our Brave Boys.*

MARIAH GALE Nurse Ludmilla

Training: Guildhall School of Music and Drama

Theatre: Credits include *Much Ado About Nothing* (Globe);*The Lost Child* (Chichester); *Stealing Sweets & Punching People* (Latchmere); *Playhouse Creatures* (Annie Castledine); *Broken* (Edinburgh); *Advent* (Birmingham Uni); *Juno and The Paycock* (USA Tour); *As You Like It, The Trojan Women, Three Sisters, Measure for Measure* and *The King of Hearts* (all for Guildhall).

TOM GODWIN Dr Oskar Bernhardi

Training: Ecole Jacques Lecoq.

Theatre: Credits include *Volpone* (Royal Exchange, Manchester); *Skylight* (Vaudeville); *Elizabeth Rex* (Birmingham Rep); *Secret Heart* (Manchester Royal Exchange); *For One Night Only* (Clod Ensemble at BAC); *Robin Hood* (Chipping Norton); *King Lear* (St Marthe, Paris); *The Fantastic Flaw* (Park Avenue Productions, Tokyo); *One* (Jamworks at Truman Brewery); *Signals of Distress* (The Flying Machine at Soho Rep, New York); *Gigantones* (Porto 2001 and international tour); and *DriveRideWalk* (Bridewell).

For Blow Up Theatre Company: *Somebody To Love* (international tour) and *The Illusion Brothers* (Total Theatre award winner 2003, Edinburgh Festival).

TV: Credits include *Waking the Dead, Grease Monkeys, Eastenders, My Dad's The Prime Minister, Anchor Me, Battleplan,* and *Sword of Honour.*

Film: *The Mourners.*

JAKE HARDERS Father Franz Reder / Dr Wenger

Training: Grotowski Center, Poland; Central School of Speech and Drama.

Theatre: Credits include *Candida* (Oxford Stage Company) – nominated for 2005 Ian Charleson Award.

TV: *The Genius of Beethoven* and *Foyle's War.*

CAROLINE HAYES Secretary / Housekeeper

Theatre: Credits include *The Real Thing* (Donmar Warehouse); *The Crucible* (Hope Theatre); *Crazyface* (Bristol Old Vic); and *Our Country's Good* (HTV Studio).

TV: Credits include *Inspector Lynley, Perfectly Frank, Servants, First Degree, Casualty, Down To Earth, Doctors, Star Hunter, The Bill, As If, The Sins, Safe as Houses, The Scarlet Pimpernel, The Tenth Kingdom, Wing and A Prayer,* and *Wavelength.*

Film: Credits include *Maybe Baby.*

Radio: Credits include *Magpie Stories* and *The Sound of Silence*.

FRED PEARSON Professor Cyprian

Theatre: Credits include *Woyzeck* (The Gate); *Serjeant Musgrave's Dance* (Oxford Stage Company); *The Prince of Homburg* (RSC/Lyric Hammersmith); *John Gabriel Borkman* (ETT and national tour); and *After the Gods* (Hampstead Theatre).

Fred has worked extensively for the National Theatre, the Royal Shakespeare Company, the Royal Court, and Joint Stock.

TV: Credits include *The Great Ship, Midsomer Murders, Hear the Silence, State of Play, As Time Goes By,* and *A&E.*

Film: *My Name is Modesty, Priest,* and *American Friends.*

DALE RAPLEY Professor Ebenwald

Training: Bristol Old Vic Theatre School.

Theatre: Credits include Bill in *Mamma Mia* (Prince Edward & Prince of Wales); Dexter in *High Society*; Oberon in *A Midsummer Night's Dream* (Regent's Park); Arnold Champion Cheney in *The Circle* (Oxford Stage Company /National tour); Snug in *A Midsummer Night's Dream* (RSC); Bluntschli in *Arms and the Man*; Charles Appelby in *Eden End* (West Yorkshire Playhouse); Leading Actor in *Six Characters* (Young Vic); Elyot in *Private Lives*, Lec in *Virtual Reality*; Valder in *A Word From Our Sponsor*; Robert in *Dreams from a Summer House*; A in *Village Wooing*; Frenchy in *Rocket to the Moon* (Stephen Joseph Theatre); The Doctor in *The Ignoramus and the Maniac* (White Bear Theatre); Peter in *Company* (Library Theatre, Manchester); Bob Cratchit in *A Christmas Carol*; Mr. Tebrick in *Lady Into Fox* (Lyric Hammersmith); Harry in *Flora the Red Menace*; Axel in *Playing with Fire* (Orange Tree Theatre); Cliff in *Cabaret* (Derby Playhouse); Jake and Mead in *Safe Sex* (Contact Theatre); Jack in *The Importance of Being Earnest* (Belgrade Theatre, Coventry); Bill Paradene in *Good Morning Bill* (Watermill Theatre, Newbury); Walker in *Prin*; Paul Bratter in *Barefoot in the Park* (Wolsey Theatre, Ipswich); Bassanio in *The Merchant of Venice* (Ludlow/Holland Park); Greek Chorus in *Philoctetes*; Sebastian in *The Tempest* (Cheek By Jowl); Dick Tassel in *The Happiest Days of Your Life*; Mortimer in *Mary Stuart*; Hastings in *She Stoops to Conquer*; Gerald in *When We Are Married* (Salisbury Playhouse); Angelo and Others in *Piaf*; Banquo in *Macbeth*; John in

The Hired Man (Royal Northampton); Clark in *Arturo Ui*; Ferdinand in *The Tempest*; The Mad Hatter in *Alice*; Valere in *Tartuffe;* and Edward in *Blood Brothers* (Swan Theatre, Worcester).

Television: Credits include *Poirot, Doctors, Spooks, Silent Witness, Aquila II, Eastenders, Casualty, Julia Jekyll and Harriet Hyde, The Peter Townsend Story, Between the Lines, The Vision Thing, Medics,* and *Birds of a Feather.*

Film: Credits include *Paper Mask.*

Radio: Credits include *The Forsyte Chronicles*, *The Beaux' Stratagem*, *Mother Courage*, *Three Sisters*, *The Vicissitudes of Evangeline,* and *Laughter in the Dark.*

JOHN STAHL Professor Pflugfelder /
His Excellency Dr Flint

Training: Royal Scottish Academy of Music and Drama.

Theatre: Credits include *Tamar's Revenge, House of Desires, Pedro The Great Pretender* (all for the RSC); *Serjeant Musgrave's Dance* (Oxford Stage Company); *Bread and Butter* (Oxford Stage Company and Dumbfounded Theatre Company); *Mr Placebo, Gagarin Way, The Meeting, Anna Weiss, Shining Souls, The Architect* (all for the Traverse Theatre, Edinburgh); *The Weir* (Royal Court Theatre tour); *The Magic Toyshop* (Shared Experience); *Crave* (Paines Plough); *Macbeth, Sleeping Beauty, Paddy's Market* and *The Real Wurld* (all for the Tron Theatre, Glasgow).

TV: Credits include *High Road, The Darien Venture, Doctors, Glasgow Kiss, Resort to Murder, Para Handy, Doctor Finlay, Taggart, You're a Good Boy, Son, Albert and the Lion* and *Crime Story.*

DEKA WALMSLEY Dr Schreimann /
Privy Counsellor Winkler / Dr Goldenthal

Training: Rose Bruford Drama School

Theatre: Credits include Finnegan in *Keepers of the Flame* (RSC); George in *Gaffer* (Southwark Playhouse / York Theatre Royal); Benny in *Bones* (Hampstead Theatre); James Jackson in *Laughter When We're Dead* (Live Theatre); *Mapping The Edge* (Wilson Wilson / Sheffield Crucible); Sidney in *News from the Seventh Floor* (Wilson Wilson / Watford); George in *Noir* (Northern Stage) *NE1* (Live Theatre); Boxer in *Animal Farm* (Northern Stage); Sammy in *Blood Brothers* (West End); and Dad in *Cooking with Elvis* (West End).

TV and Film: Credits include Ed in *55 degrees North*, Tarawicz in *Rebus: The Hanging Garden*, David in *Like Father*, Tom in *Dirty War*, Captain Marchant in *Waking the Dead*, Harry in *Ticket to Ride*, Eddy in *Wallpaper Warrior* and Stuart in *Singing the Blues*.

Radio: Credits include *The Taming of the Shrew* (Radio 4), *A Midsummer Night's Dream* (Radio 4), *The H File* (Radio 3), *The Spire* (Radio 4), *Callum* (Radio 4), *City at Night* (Radio 4), *Laughter When We're Dead* (Radio 3) and *Snapper* (Radio 4).

Writer

ARTHUR SCHNITZLER

Arthur Schnitzler was born in 1862 in Vienna. He worked as a practising doctor until 1894 when he retired and devoted his energy to writing as part of the 1890's 'Vienna group', known for their concentration on psychological dramas about contemporary Viennese society. As a doctor he was fascinated by psychiatry and was a keen follower of Freud.

His works are characterised by their pitiless analyses of human relationships and motivations, and people's inbuilt fear of death. Plays such as *Anatol* (1893, *Affairs of Anatol*, 1911) and *Reigon* (1897, *Merry-go-round*, 1953), set in the decadent and romanticised city of Vienna, explore relationships between the sexes while other plays such as *Professor Bernhardi* (1912 *trans*. 1927) express the anti-Semitism prevalent in contemporary society.

As he grew older Schnitzler became obsessed with old age and death, for instance in his novel *Beatrice* (1913). His ideas challenged contemporary bourgeois morality, and as a result he was forced to endure a measure of abuse during his life. His work also suffered under the Nazi regime due to his pro-Semitic themes and his exigent explorations of human psychology. He is one of Austria's most famous playwrights and wrote twenty three full length plays, ten one-act plays and many prose works. He died in Vienna in 1931.

Creative Team

SAMUEL ADAMSON Adaptor

Samuel Adamson's plays include *Southwark Fair,* a new version of Ibsen's *Pillars of the Community*, and *Mrs Affleck* (from Ibsen's *Little Eyolf*) at the National Theatre, as well as *Frank & Ferdinand* for National Theatre Connections. He is Artistic Associate on the Tony award-winning stage adaptation of Michael Morpurgo's *War Horse* (Lincoln Center Theater, New York and Princess of Wales Theatre, Toronto). Other plays and adaptations include: *Boston Manor* (Theatre 503/Theatre Voice), *Fish and Company* (Soho Theatre/National Youth Theatre), *Clocks and Whistles* (Bush Theatre and New York, Time Out award), *Drink, Dance, Laugh and Lie* (Bush/Channel 4), *Grace Note* (Peter Hall Company/Old Vic), *Some Kind of Bliss* (Trafalgar Studios and Brits Off Broadway, New York), *Tomorrow Week* (BBC Radio 3); as well as contributions to *24 Hour Plays* (Old Vic), *A Chain Play* (Almeida) and *Decade* (Headlong). His play of *All About My Mother* (from Pedro Almodóvar's film; Old Vic Theatre; 2008 Whatsonstage Theatregoers' Choice Best New Play) has been translated into many languages and is performed regularly around the world. Versions include: Chekhov's *The Cherry Orchard* (Oxford Stage Company/ Riverside Studios), *Three Sisters* (OSC tour and West End), Ibsen's *A Doll's House* (Southwark Playhouse, Northcott Theatre Exeter and Dundee Rep), Bernhard Studlar's *Transdanubia Dreaming* (National Theatre Studio) and Ostrovsky's *Larissa and the Merchants* (Insite Performance Company). Film: *Running for River* (Directional Studios/ Krug). He was writer in residence at the Bush Theatre in 1997-8.

MARK ROSENBLATT Director

Mark is Artistic Director of Dumbfounded Theatre for whom he has directed CP Taylor's *Bread and Butter* at Southwark Playhouse, in a subsequent touring revival (co-produced with Oxford Stage Company) and at the Tricycle Theatre in 2004 (also with OSC).
Freelance work includes *The Taming of the Shrew* (Thelma Holt Ltd / Plymouth Theatre Royal and National tour); *The Tempest* (National Theatre tour and Cottesloe); W Somerset Maugham's *The Circle* (for Oxford Stage Company and Salisbury Playhouse); two subsequent revivals of *The Circle*, one for Oxford Stage Company and one as a commercial tour starring Wendy Craig and Tony Britton (TEG / Yvonne Arnaud, Guildford); Kay Mellor's *A Passionate Woman* (Northampton Theatres); his own adaptation of S Anski's *The Dybbuk* (BAC) for which he received the James Menzies-Kitchin Young Director Award in 1999. Mark also directed BAFTA-nominated recordings of Shakespeare's *Romeo and Juliet, Hamlet, A Midsummer Night's Dream* and *Macbeth* for Kartouche Audio.

JON BAUSOR Designer

Jon read Music as a choral scholar at Oxford University and studied at Exeter College of Art before training on the Motley Theatre Design Course. He was a finalist in the Linbury Prize for Stage Design 2000. Recent theatre designs include *Frankenstein* (Derby Playhouse); *Bread and Butter* (Tricycle Theatre); *Sanctuary The Tempest* (National Theatre); W*inners, Interior, The Exception and the Rule, The New Tenant, The Soul of Chien-Nu Leaves her Body* (Young Vic); *The Taming of the Shrew* (Theatre Royal Plymouth / Thelma Holt Ltd); *Tartuffe, Ghosts in the Cottonwoods* (Arcola); *The America Play* (RADA); *Switchback, Possible Worlds* (Tron Theatre); *The Tempest* and *What the Women Did* (Southwark Playhouse).

Dance designs include *Before the Tempest...After the Storm, Sophie/ Stateless* (Linbury, ROH); *Mixtures* (ENB / Westminster Abbey); *Non Exeunt* (Ballet Boyz/ Sadlers Wells).

Design for opera includes *The Queen of Spades* (Edinburgh Festival Theatre); *Cosi Fan Tutti* (British tour) and *King Arthur* (New Chamber Opera).

Forthcoming work includes *The Knot Garden* (Neue Oper Vienna); *Cymbeline* (Regent's Park); *In the Bag* (Traverse) and *Ghosts* (Linbury, ROH).

TIM MASCALL Lighting Designer

Recent lighting design credits include: *Vote Dizzy!* (Soho Theatre, London); *Why The Whales Came* (Comedy Theatre, London); *Off The Wall* (David Glass Ensemble UK Tour); *Filler Up!* (London, Washington DC, Montreal); *Passion* (Marie Forbes Dance Co, The Place Theatre, London); *Dazed* (Fracture Dance Theatre, Bloomsbury Theatre, London); *Testify* and *Cloudscape* (Middlesex University Dance Department); *The Sports Show 2004 / Main Arena* (Earl's Court, London); *When Harry Met Barry* (The Venue, London).

As an Associate Lighting Designer, Tim has worked with Chris Davey on *The Vagina Monologues* (UK tours and West End) and Matthew Eagland on *Little Women* (The Duchess Theatre, London).

Re-lights have included: *Home* (UK tour Oxford Stage Company); *My Boy Jack* (UK tour, Kenneth Wax Ltd / Hague Lang Productions); *The Lieutenant Of Inishmore* (UK tour); *Hay Fever* (UK tour, Oxford Stage Company); *Unheimlich Spine* (The David Glass Ensemble); *Plunge, To Time Taking Blush, She is as He Eats, Inside Somewhere, Cranes, Playfall* and *Interlock* (all for Scottish Dance Theatre / Dundee Rep Theatre).

Other credits include sound designs for *After The Dance* (UK tour, Oxford Stage Company / Salisbury Playhouse), *The Cherry Orchard* (UK tour, Oxford Stage Company), *The Seagull, The Cherry Orchard,* and *The Futurists* (Drama Centre London).

ADRIENNE QUARTLY Sound Designer

Having studied music and become a Radio Producer for 5 years, Adrienne then gained a Master's Degree in Sound Design / Music for Performance at Central School of Speech and Drama in 2002. She now works as a freelance creative sound designer/composer in London. Productions include Quiconque's *Hideaway* (Complicité); *Lady Luck* (Lucy Porter at Assembly Rooms, Edinburgh 04); *Donkey Haughty* and *Attempts on Her Life* (BAC); *Jarman Garden* and *3 Women* (Riverside Studios); *Forgotten Voices* (Southwark Playhouse); *Habeas Corpus* and *Quartermaine's Terms* (Royal Theatre Northampton and Salisbury Playhouse); Circo Ridiculoso's *Inflated Ideas* (National Circus Bites Tour); *The Increased Difficulty of Concentration* and, most recently, *Woyzeck* and *Tejas Verdes* (Gate Theatre). Operating includes *Dumb Show* (Royal Court). As a cellist she is featured on Piano Magic's album *Artists Rifles*.

SALLYANN DICKSEE Costume Supervisor

Sallyann studied tailoring and pattern cutting at the London College of Fashion and took her first job at the Royal Opera House as a tailor and cutter. Following that she became a freelance wardrobe mistress and costume supervisor.
Theatre credits include *Mamma Mia* (London and Stuttgart); *His Dark Materials* (National Theatre); *Art* (David Pugh Ltd); *Life x 3* (David Pugh Ltd); *Up for Grabs* (Wyndhams Theatre) and *A Passionate Woman* (Comedy Theatre).
Music credits include *Bond*, *Geri Halliwell*.
Film & TV credits include *Clandestine Marriage*, *Harry Potter III*, *Stage Beauty*, *Pride and Prejudice*, *Vera Drake* and *Turn of the Screw* (BBC Wales).

LYDIA ZIEMKE Assistant Director

Lydia has recently completed LAMDA's directing programme, and has just finished assisting Daniel Kramer on *Woyzeck* at the Gate Theatre, London. After living and working in Berlin, she moved to Edinburgh and in 2000 co-founded a Studio Ensemble at the Guilded Balloon. There she produced, directed and designed 2 seasons of productions concentrating on European scripts from young writers. Of these, *Like Skinnydipping* (co-directed with the author), won the Award for best new play and best direction at the National Student Drama Festival, 2003.

ANNA JONES Assistant Designer

Anna trained on the Motley Theatre Design course. Since graduating last summer she has designed *The Biggleswades* at Southwark Playhouse, and assisted other designers including work on: *Tartuffe* (Arcola: designed by Jon Bausor); *Woyzeck* (Gate: designed by Neil Irish); and *A Night Just Before The Forest* (Arcola: designed by Patrick Burnier). Prior to Motley Anna studied drama at The University of Hull where she designed *The Hairy Ape, Weldon Rising* and *Puck.*

TOM ROGERS Assistant Designer

Following a Drama degree at Bristol University, Tom trained at Motley. Since graduating in July 2004, design work includes: Britten's *Let's Make An Opera / The Little Sweep* with director Will Kerley at the Benjamin Britten Festival, Aldeburgh; new opera *To the Edge* at the Steiner Theatre, Baker Street; *The Chimes* at Southwark Playhouse with artistic director Gareth Machin, and *Death and The Maiden* at the New Wolsey, Ipswich. He has assisted director David Edwards on Engelbert Humperdinck's *Hansel and Gretel* at the Proms 2004. Future projects include: Peter Brook's *The Man Who* at The Orange Tree, Richmond, and a touring production of Nick Darke's new play, *Laughing Gas*.

CHRIS UMNEY Production Manager

Since graduating from the Visual and Performing Arts (Theatre) BA course at Brighton University in 1995 Chris has been working as a composer, sound engineer, lighting designer and production manager for performance companies both in the UK and in Europe.
He has toured the UK with numerous companies including Sound & Fury, The People Show, Trio Con Brio, Voodoo Vaudeville, Quirk Productions, Bandbazi, Bright FX, Facepack Theatre, Intoto Theatre, Clout Dance Theatre, Barb Jungr and Brighton Theatre Events.
From 1994 to 1998 he was fortunate to work throughout Europe with the Brighton based Divas Dance Theatre Company and in 2001 Chris toured to 24 theatres in The Netherlands with Swamp Circus Theatre's production of *Moto*.
Most recently he worked as Production Manager on BAC's Christmas show *World Cup Final 1966* and designed the lighting for High Spin's touring performances of *Whodunnit?* and *Sleepwalker*, seen at the Hackney Empire in September 2004.

NEIL LAIDLAW Producer – Last Waltz Season

Neil is Producer for Dumbfounded Theatre and first worked with Mark Rosenblatt on the touring production of *Bread and Butter*. Originally from Scotland, he trained at the Royal Scottish Academy of Music and Drama. He has worked for many Scottish theatre companies, including Theatre by Design in their production of *Ghost Shirt* (Tron Theatre / Edinburgh Fringe) and Theatre Informer's Scottish tour of *Oleanna* by David Mamet. In 2002, he was awarded the prestigious Theatre Investment Fund / Society of London Theatre New Producers Bursary which allowed him to develop various projects over the year. Neil has most recently worked with Renard Company in a production at Glasgow's Tramway Theatre, and with early years theatre company Licketyspit. Neil is also producer for NML Productions, who recently co-produced *Sweet Phoebe* at the Byre Theatre, St Andrews.

Oxford Stage Company

'Oxford Stage Company has been one of the great success stories of recent years' The Daily Telegraph

Oxford Stage Company enjoys the freedom to produce work of great variety in a great variety of venues. From Stirling to the West End, we produce anything from drawing room classics to ambitious new plays. Our constant standard is to produce powerful and accomplished work that affects audiences anywhere, to return neglected classics to the popular repertoire and to present our work with wit and imagination and passion. We are also committed to giving opportunities to young artists and theatre workers, and to helping them increase their store of knowledge and experience. We are delighted by the opportunity to co-produce **The Last Waltz Season** at the Arcola. It fulfils all of our objectives. It also affords a wonderful insight into the hopes and the failings of Western Europe a hundred years ago.

Our goal is to develop a consistently exciting education and access programme to accompany our tours and to continue giving the best young directors, designers and actors an opportunity to work on a challenging larger scale.

Like most other arts organisations, we need to look for funding from every source to ensure that we thrive and grow. You can help us build on our vision to produce bold, timeless and relevant theatre by joining our Friends Scheme. Great theatre can only happen with Friends like you. With your support, we'll achieve even more.

If you would like to join our free mailing list or our friends scheme please contact us by phone on 020 7438 9946 or via email at info@oxford-stage.co.uk

For more information on future productions please go to our website www.oxfordstage.co.uk

Artistic Director	Dominic Dromgoole
Executive Producer	Henny Finch
Development Producer	Julia Hallawell
Associate Director	Sean Holmes
Finance and Administration Manager	Helen Hillman
Production and Tour Manager	Stephen Pamplin
Education Associate	Jacqui Somerville
Marketing and Administrative Assistant	Becky Pepper

OSC would like to thank all our Friends and especially our Favourites:
Muriel E B Quinn, John and Margaret Lynch and Uncle Honza.

Oxford Stage Company
Chertsey Chambers
12 Mercer Street
London WC2H 9QD

020 7438 9940
info@oxfordstage.co.uk

Dumbfounded Theatre

Dumbfounded Theatre is a young company committed to the rediscovery of neglected work by outstanding European writers. Led by Mark Rosenblatt (Artistic Director) and Neil Laidlaw (Producer) it was formed in 2001 to stage a highly successful production of C P Taylor's *Bread and Butter* at Southwark Playhouse. *Bread and Butter* was subsequently revived in a touring co-production with Oxford Stage Company, and again at The Tricycle Theatre in 2004.

Future Projects: *Passages*

Samuel Adamson's newly commissioned play *Passages* (working title) intertwines three short stories by Nobel Prize-winning Yiddish novelist Isaac Bashevis Singer. *Passages* is being developed for production later this year.

Dumbfounded Theatre receives no core funding from Arts Council England or any other source. We raise funds on a project-to-project basis. We rely on the support of companies and individuals to allow us to develop our future plans. If you can help in any way please contact Neil Laidlaw on 020 8911 9276 or via email at info@dumbfounded.co.uk

Dumbfounded Theatre
60 Fellows Road
London NW3 3LJ
020 8911 9276 / 020 7483 2582
0870 460 1483 (f)
www.dumbfounded.co.uk

Contents

* See 'A note on this version' on page 5.

PROFESSOR BERNHARDI
A Comedy in Five Acts

First published in this version in 2005 by Oberon Books Ltd
521 Caledonian Road, London N7 9RH
Tel: +44 (0) 20 7607 3637 / Fax: +44 (0) 20 7607 3629
e-mail: info@oberonbooks.com
www.oberonbooks.com

A catalogue record for this book is available from the British
Library.

ISBN: 9781840025521

Cover design: Pansy Aung and Winnie Wong

Characters

At the Imperial Ministry of Education and Cultural Affairs:

HIS EXCELLENCY DR FLINT
Minister for Education and Cultural Affairs

PRIVY COUNSELLOR* WINKLER

SECRETARY

From the Church of St Florian:

FATHER FRANZ REDER
Priest

Representing Bernhardi:

DR GOLDENTHAL

At Bernhardi's Home:

HOUSEKEEPER

** An honorary title conferred on a senior civil servant for
distinguished service.*

Act One

The modest ante-room to a ward at the Elisabeth Institute, a private teaching hospital, Vienna, c.1900. One door leads to the ward, another to a corridor. A table; chairs; cupboard; shelves with test-tubes and bottles; books, patients' records and magazines; coat-stand; old photograph of the professors. NURSE LUDMILLA (late twenties; quite pretty, pale; large eyes) is busy at the shelves. From the ward, enter MR HOCHROITZPOINTNER (student of medicine; twenty-five; medium height, plump, pale, duelling scar, neat moustache, chic hair; pince-nez).

HOCHROITZPOINTNER: Professor not here yet? Taking their time down there. (*He opens a folder.*) Three autopsies in a week. For a ward of twenty beds that's unheard of – and we'll have a fourth tomorrow.

NURSE LUDMILLA: You think, Mr Hochroitzpointner – the sepsis?

HOCHROITZPOINTNER: (*Nodding.*) Mmn. Police report finished?

NURSE LUDMILLA: Yes, Mr Hochroitzpointner.

HOCHROITZPOINTNER: Can't prove it, but it was definitely an abortion. Grisly world out there, Nurse Ludmilla. (*He sees a parcel on the table.*) Ah, the invitations – about time! 'The Elisabeth Institute Annual Ball. Princess Stixenstein, patroness...' Are you coming?

NURSE LUDMILLA: (*Smiling.*) I don't think so, Mr Hochroitzpointner.

HOCHROITZPOINTNER: Oh – dancing not allowed?

NURSE LUDMILLA: We're not a religious order – nothing's forbidden.

HOCHROITZPOINTNER: (*Looking at her slyly.*) Truly? Nothing at all?

27

NURSE LUDMILLA: Anyway, nurses don't really have the flair for it.

HOCHROITZPOINTNER: Why not? If doctors have it. Look at Dr Adler, he's got lashings of panache, and he carves up dead bodies all day. I tell you, I'm on top of the world at an autopsy.

From the corridor, enter DR OSKAR BERNHARDI (assistant to PROFESSOR BERNHARDI; twenty-five; elegant, considerate, slightly unsure of himself).

OSKAR: Good morning.

HOCHROITZPOINTNER: Morning.

OSKAR: Father won't be long.

HOCHROITZPOINTNER: All finished down there? What did they discover? – if you don't mind me asking.

OSKAR: The tumour started in the kidney and was distinctly defined.

HOCHROITZPOINTNER: So we might have operated?

OSKAR: *Might*, yes.

HOCHROITZPOINTNER: If Professor Ebenwald had seen eye-to-eye with Professor Bern –

OSKAR: – we'd have had the autopsy a week ago. Oh – the ball invitations!

HOCHROITZPOINTNER: Affair of the season, the papers are full of it. And I've heard on the grapevine, Oskar, you've composed 'The Elisabeth Institute Waltz' in honour of the Board –

OSKAR: (*Waving this aside.*) Yes, yes. (*He nods towards the ward.*) What's new in there?

HOCHROITZPOINTNER: Sepsis girl – it won't be long.

OSKAR: Oh… (*Sadly.*) Nothing to be done.

HOCHROITZPOINTNER: I gave her some camphor.

From the corridor, enter PROFESSOR BERNHARDI (Professor of Internal Medicine and Director of the Institute; OSKAR's father; fifties; grey beard, neat hair; overcoat; frank, more like a man of the world than a scholar) and his first assistant DR KURT PFLUGFELDER (twenty-seven; moustache; pince-nez; chipper but serious). NURSE LUDMILLA takes BERNHARDI's coat and hangs it up.

KURT: …no, I have to say it, professor: Dr Adler wanted Professor *Ebenwald*'s diagnosis to be the right one.

BERNHARDI: (*Smiling.*) Stop sniffing out treason, Dr Pflugfelder – it's no good for you, you know.

HOCHROITZPOINTNER: Good morning, Professor Bernhardi.

BERNHARDI: Good morning.

HOCHROITZPOINTNER: Just heard from Dr Oskar that we got it right.

BERNHARDI: Yes – though 'we' got it wrong as well, or don't you sit in on Professor Ebenwald's lectures these days?

OSKAR: Mr Hochroitzpointner sits in on lectures in every department.

BERNHARDI: Then you must have a healthy stockpile of allegiances.

HOCHROITZPOINTNER narrows his lips. BERNHARDI taps a hand on his shoulder amiably.

What's new?

HOCHROITZPOINTNER: The sepsis is in a very bad way.

BERNHARDI: Still alive? Poor thing.

He signs several papers for NURSE LUDMILLA.

KURT: They might as well have kept her in gynaecology.

OSKAR: No free beds.

HOCHROITZPOINTNER: What are we going to record as the cause of death?

OSKAR: Sepsis – what do you think?

HOCHROITZPOINTNER: Yes, and the cause of the sepsis? Because it probably was a…backstreet operation –

BERNHARDI: We can't prove that. No evidence of injury. We've written a police report, and for us, it's over. Just as it was for the unlucky girl days ago. (*He heads for the ward.*)

Enter PROFESSOR EBENWALD (Professor of Surgery and Vice-Director of the Institute; forty-ish; tall, lean, full beard; spectacles, overcoat; vocally slightly pompous, overstated).

EBENWALD: Good morning, is – ah, there's our Director.

BERNHARDI: Morning, Ebenwald.

EBENWALD: Could you spare a few seconds? (*Confidentially.*) Professor Tugendvetter's department. We should have a chat about his successor.

BERNHARDI: Oh, that can wait, can't it? Half an hour? My office?

EBENWALD: I'm afraid I have a class then, Bernhardi.

BERNHARDI: (*Considering this.*) I won't be long. Give me a moment?

EBENWALD: Certainly.

BERNHARDI: (*To OSKAR.*) The autopsy notes for Mr Hochroitzpointner?

OSKAR: Oh, yes. (*He takes them out of his pocket and gives them to HOCHROITZPOINTNER.*) If you could enter them straight away, please?

HOCHROITZPOINTNER: Naturally.

BERNHARDI, OSKAR, KURT and NURSE LUDMILLA exit to the ward. HOCHROITZPOINTNER sits and prepares to write. EBENWALD approaches the window and wipes his spectacles.

(*Assiduously.*) You don't want to sit while you wait, Professor Ebenwald?

EBENWALD: I'm not here, Hochroitzpointner. Everything all right with you?

HOCHROITZPOINTNER: (*Standing.*) Well, professor, exams, you know… My last *viva* is in a few weeks and things are slightly… It's pandemonium, frankly.

EBENWALD: You're the kind who romps through life – I can't see a problem.

HOCHROITZPOINTNER: I *am* pretty confident, in terms of practice, professor. It's just all the 'grey' theory, as Goethe puts it. Bores me stiff.

EBENWALD: Hmn. It wasn't my favourite thing, either. (*Confidentially.*) This'll perk you up, I flunked physiology. It doesn't necessarily harm a career, does it?

HOCHROITZPOINTNER laughs delightedly and sits.

Autopsy notes?

HOCHROITZPOINTNER: Yes.

EBENWALD: Great celebrations in Israel, hmn?

HOCHROITZPOINTNER: (*Uncertainly.*) I...I don't
follow, professor.

EBENWALD: Well – Bernhardi's department.
Diagnostically victorious.

HOCHROITZPOINTNER: Oh, you mean because the
tumour was defined?

EBENWALD: Yes, and originated in the kidney.

HOCHROITZPOINTNER: It was, I think, a guess...a
good guess...

EBENWALD: A guess, Mr Hochroitzpointner? Are you
non compos mentis? It was diagnostic knack! Doctor's gut
instinct!

HOCHROITZPOINTNER: And it *was* inoperable.

EBENWALD: Oh, an operation was out of the question.
Hospitals can afford such novel things; *we're* a young
private institute. But don't mind me.

HOCHROITZPOINTNER writes.

Apologies. One more thing. You sit in on lectures in
Professor Tugendvetter's department, do you?

HOCHROITZPOINTNER: Yes, professor.

EBENWALD: Tell me, what are Dr Wenger's lectures like?

HOCHROITZPOINTNER: Dr Wenger?

EBENWALD: You know, when he stands in for old
Tugendvetter – if *he's* called to a fox-hunt or a prince
with the snuffles?

HOCHROITZPOINTNER: Oh. Yes, then Dr Wenger
would lecture for Professor Tugendvetter.

EBENWALD: And? Quite confidential.

HOCHROITZPOINTNER: (*Uncertainly.*) He's, he's...
good. He's...perky. A bit over-erudite, I suppose you'd
say. I shouldn't be talking about a future boss.

EBENWALD: What do you mean? No decision on that
score. Plenty of other candidates. Anyway, this is
between us...could be a friendly conversation over a
tankard. *Vox populi, vox dei.* What specifically have you
got against Dr Wenger?

HOCHROITZPOINTNER: Well...it's not so much his
lectures I don't like...it's more his whole attitude. He is
a bit arrogant.

EBENWALD: True to type, hmn? Lacks inherent modesty?
A 'big-mouthed outlander', as my cousin in the Lower
House would say?

HOCHROITZPOINTNER: Oh, that's good...'big-
mouthed outlander'... (*Encouraged.*) He does speak in his
particular jargon, does Dr Wenger...

EBENWALD: In Austria there are many dialects. It
shouldn't matter, should it?

*BERNHARDI, OSKAR, KURT and NURSE LUDMILLA
enter from the ward.*

BERNHARDI: All yours, Ebenwald.

*NURSE LUDMILLA presents him with another document
to sign.*

Hmn? Oh. (*To EBENWALD.*) Excuse me again. (*As he
signs.*) It never fails to amaze me. (*To EBENWALD.*) The
sepsis girl. Eighteen. Wide awake. She wants to get out
of bed, she thinks she's in the pink of health. And her
pulse barely registers, it could be over in the hour.

EBENWALD: (*Professionally.*) It's very common, isn't it?

HOCHROITZPOINTNER: (*Assiduously.*) More camphor,
perhaps?

BERNHARDI: (*Looking at him calmly.*) You could have spared her the first shot. (*Reassuring him.*) Maybe the sweetest hour of her life is down to you. Though I know that wasn't quite what you intended.

HOCHROITZPOINTNER: (*Irritated.*) Why do you say that, professor? I'm not a butcher, am I?

BERNHARDI: Did I accuse you of such a thing?

HOCHROITZPOINTNER and EBENWALD exchange a glance.

(*To NURSE LUDMILLA.*) Relatives?

NURSE LUDMILLA: She hasn't had a single visitor.

BERNHARDI: Her lover?

KURT: *He's* not likely to show his face here. (*He busies himself at the shelves.*)

OSKAR: She probably doesn't even know his name.

BERNHARDI: So this is love. Well, Ebenwald, now I'm yours.

OSKAR: Father, will you check in on her again? She begged me to ask you.

BERNHARDI: Yes.

OSKAR has a word to KURT, and they return to the ward.

NURSE LUDMILLA: (*To HOCHROITZPOINTNER.*) I'll fetch the priest.

HOCHROITZPOINTNER: Yes, why not? No real tragedy if you're too late, though.

NURSE LUDMILLA exits. HOCHROITZPOINTNER takes some patients' notes and exits to the ward.

EBENWALD: (*Having become quite impatient.*) Well, Bernhardi, here's the thing. I've just received a letter from Dr Hell in Graz – and he's happy to consider succeeding Professor Tugendvetter.

BERNHARDI: Oh he is, is he? Someone's mentioned it to him, then?

EBENWALD: I took the liberty – we were students together, he's an old friend.

BERNHARDI: I assume you wrote to him off the record?

EBENWALD: Of course – no decision's been made, has it? All the same, as Vice-Director, I thought it appropriate – especially as Tugendvetter himself agrees that Dr Hell's a fine prospect.

BERNHARDI: (*Quite sharply.*) Tugendvetter isn't leaving the Institute till the start of the summer semester. Therefore this conversation, and, I have to say, your correspondence with Dr Hell, are premature. What's the rush? – especially as Tugendvetter's present assistant, Dr Wenger, has proved himself more than capable of deputising – more than once.

EBENWALD: Could I say now, Bernhardi, I'm not fond of makeshift arrangements...

From the corridor enter PROFESSOR TUGENDVETTER (Professor of Dermatology and Syphilis; fifty-ish; grey, side-burns; hat; more like a stockbroker than a scholar; blithe, deliberately jocular, though in need of approval). He takes off his hat.

TUGENDVETTER: Morning all. Hello, Bernhardi, been looking for you. Hello, Ebenwald.

EBENWALD: I'm in the way –

TUGENDVETTER: Don't be silly. Nothing classified here. (*To BERNHARDI.*) Right. Here it is: the Minister for Education's asked if I'd be able to take over down at the clinic straight away. ASAP.

BERNHARDI: How do you know this?

TUGENDVETTER: I was at the Ministry yesterday and saw the Minister – they want to build me a super new wing, you know – he said to say hi, by the way –

BERNHARDI: Who?

TUGENDVETTER: The Minister.

BERNHARDI: Flint?

TUGENDVETTER: (*Nodding.*) Wouldn't shut up about you. Thinks the world of you. Fellow students, eager assistants, salad days. His words. What a career. The first time a clinical professor's ever become Minister for Education, at least in Austria.

BERNHARDI: Mmn, very shrewd politician, your new friend Flint.

TUGENDVETTER: He has a real interest in your Institute. *Our* Institute – still here, aren't I?

BERNHARDI: So interested he wanted to wipe it out, once.

TUGENDVETTER: Oh, that wasn't him, that was the whole Doctors' Society. Old guard against the new, all forgotten. I swear, Bernhardi, Flint holds the Institute in high esteem.

BERNHARDI: Thank God we can *just* about get by without that. The question is, Professor Tugendvetter, how did you answer him?

TUGENDVETTER: Well, it isn't up to me, is it! (*Humorously.*) *That* is up to my chief!

BERNHARDI: We wouldn't want to keep you against your will. Happily, you have a talented assistant who can fill your shoes in the short term.

TUGENDVETTER: Young Wenger, eh? Able lad. You don't want him to get too comfy, though.

EBENWALD: I've just said we should avoid makeshift arrangements if possible... I also mentioned a letter I've received from Dr Hell in Graz, who'd be prepared –

TUGENDVETTER: Ditto! – he wrote to me!

BERNHARDI: When can we expect publication of his *Collected Letters*?

TUGENDVETTER: (*Glancing briefly at EBENWALD.*) Bernhardi, the Institute would be lucky to have Dr Hell.

BERNHARDI: Then Graz has done wonders for the man. He wasn't thought up to much when he was in Vienna.

TUGENDVETTER: Who thought that?

BERNHARDI: You. Anyway, what you're saying is you'd rather propose Dr Hell as your successor than your own assistant?

TUGENDVETTER: Mine's a sapling. And I don't think he's even thought of it himself.

BERNHARDI: He's being modest. His latest work on serum is getting a lot of attention.

EBENWALD: A meretricious hoo-ha, Bernhardi.

TUGENDVETTER: Certainly the man's gifted. Anyway, I can't stop anyone from putting himself forward as a candidate.

BERNHARDI: The point is you'll have to choose one or the other. Hell, or Wenger.

TUGENDVETTER: Oh, no! I don't nominate my successor! Do I?

BERNHARDI: You'll take part in the vote. If you're still concerned for the Institute's future.

TUGENDVETTER: Steady on! We built it out of nothing, didn't we, the two of us, with Cyprian? Fifteen years, hmn? Here, listen, Bernhardi, what if I stayed on *and* worked at the clinic –

BERNHARDI: (*Resolutely.*) The day you start there is the day Dr Wenger stands in for you.

EBENWALD: Then I suggest an urgent meeting about the definitive filling of the post.

BERNHARDI: Anyone would think we were doing everything in our power to prevent Dr Wenger from proving his teaching ability.

EBENWALD: We're a private teaching hospital, not a finishing school for lecturers.

BERNHARDI: Leave it to me, Ebenwald. We don't drag our feet here, do we? Nor do we run recklessly.

EBENWALD: Please don't insinuate I'm asking for the latter, Bernhardi.

BERNHARDI: (*Smiling.*) Understood.

EBENWALD: (*Looking at his watch.*) Duty calls. Gentlemen.

BERNHARDI: Yes, your students. I must go as well. After you.

Enter DR ADLER (Lecturer in Pathological Anatomy; thirty-ish; fresh face, bright eyes, short, swarthy, duelling scar; overcoat; animated). EBENWALD bumps into him at the door.

EBENWALD: Morning.

He exits.

ADLER: Hello.

BERNHARDI: Curious turn-up: Dr Adler in the land of the living?

ADLER: Pity you weren't just down on Cyprian's ward. Fascinating. Nascent tumour in the cerebellum and, aside from the tabes, no symptoms.

OSKAR enters from the ward.

OSKAR: Hello, professor.

TUGENDVETTER: Mozart! No need to tell me, Oskar, know already: a new waltz for the Board!

BERNHARDI: What?

TUGENDVETTER: Subtitled, 'With a Rapid Pulse,' – d'you get it?!

OSKAR: Professor, please…

BERNHARDI: More scribbling? You've kept that quiet.

OSKAR: I have to go to the laboratory.

BERNHARDI: *(Pulling him jokingly by the ear.)* So do I, doctor, so do I…

TUGENDVETTER: Fathers and sons, eh? *Allegro ma non troppo*, gentlemen…!

BERNHARDI, OSKAR and TUGENDVETTER exit. HOCHROITZPOINTNER enters from the ward.

HOCHROITZPOINTNER: Hello, Dr Adler.

ADLER: Hello…you. Could I have a quick glance at the Bernhardi kidney-tumour decease notes?

HOCHROITZPOINTNER: Yes…certainly. *(He takes a sheet out of a folder.)*

ADLER: Thank you, Mr Hoch – Hoch – whatever you are.

HOCHROITZPOINTNER: Hochroitzpointner.

ADLER: *(Sitting.)* Quite a mouthful that, isn't it?

HOCHROITZPOINTNER: You don't like it?

ADLER: (*Looking over the notes.*) Oh, simply superb. I see mountain summits, tours of glaciers. No albumin?

HOCHROITZPOINTNER: No. He was examined every day.

KURT comes out of the ward.

KURT: Actually there was a lot of albumin the last few days.

HOCHROITZPOINTNER: Yes, that's true, albumin in the last few days, true.

ADLER: Oh yes: so it says: right here.

HOCHROITZPOINTNER: Yes. It does. Right there.

ADLER: (*To KURT.*) How's your father? Never shows his face at my post-mortems anymore. (*At the notes; to HOCHROITZPOINTNER.*) Patient only with you a week?

HOCHROITZPOINTNER: Yes. He was with Professor Ebenwald before that, but because the case was inoperable –

ADLER: (*To KURT.*) First-rate diagnostician, your boss, whatever else you might say.

KURT: (*Smiling.*) What else might you say?

ADLER: (*Rather sweetly.*) Don't jump down my throat, Dr Pflugfelder. I just mean Professor Bernhardi's department's forte is diagnosis… When it comes to treatment, you do a hell of a lot of experimenting.

KURT: What else should we do, Dr Adler, up here in internal medicine? We have to try new things, don't we?

ADLER: Oh, all this stabbing about in the dark – ruddy

irritating. That's why I hot-footed it to anatomy. One has supreme control there. (*At the case-notes.*) An x-ray as well?

KURT: You still answer to Professor Bernhardi, Dr Adler, even in anatomy.

ADLER: Much too busy to worry about me below stairs. Really, Kurt, I'm no critic of Bernhardi's.

KURT: I know. He's got plenty of them, though. Most of them green-eyed.

ADLER: The man has nothing to moan about. Practice extending to the Imperial Family. Professor. Director of the Institute.

KURT: He built it out of nothing – and who else is there?

ADLER: Quite right. And that he's done as well as he has given today's, err, climate – a climate I've a right to talk about: I've never made any bones about my Jewish descent. Though on my mother's side I'm from an old bourgeois Viennese family. Even got an undergraduate scar, duelling for the Nationalists.

KURT: Common knowledge, doctor.

ADLER: It's sweet, Kurt, how keen you are to jump to our Director's defence. For a student dueller – for a young German Nationalist – it's really something.

KURT: Spot on, Dr Adler. And I was an anti-Semite. Still am one, on the whole. But I've also become anti-Aryan. My rule is, everybody's flawed. I find the exceptions and stick to them.

Enter PROFESSOR CYPRIAN (Professor of Neuropathy; old; short; long hair, still quite blond; drawling, singsong speech, prone to sudden lecturing).

CYPRIAN: Hello, gentlemen.

They greet him.

Ah, Adler. We can take it as read that today's skull won't go walkabout, like the one that used to belong to the paralytic?

ADLER: My assistant's under strict instructions.

CYPRIAN: Your assistant's vanished. On the booze again. I'd keep an eye on him if I were you. When I was working in Prague, there was a winebibbing assistant in anatomy who crept about unstopping all the test-tubes and quaffing their contents.

ADLER: Mine's quite at home with schnapps.

BERNHARDI and OSKAR enter.

BERNHARDI: Hello, Cyprian, after me?

CYPRIAN: No, Adler, as it happens, but as you're here. I've had a thought. I wonder, might you find some time to come to the Ministry of Education with me?

They are standing together. OSKAR exits to the ward. The others talk amongst themselves.

I think we can secure something for the Institute. The fact is the new Minister's a doctor...so shouldn't we get in there and see what we can squeeze out of him?

BERNHARDI: Very optimistic of you...

CYPRIAN: Oh, I don't think so. I know Flint of old – foretold him his political career. Administrative genius. I've worked it all out. Firstly, we ask for a government subsidy – we're too yoked to these iffy private benefactors. Secondly –

BERNHARDI: Cyprian, Flint is our nemesis! It seems to have slipped your mind that when we started he concocted so many vile rumours about us we nearly went under. We were founded to steal income from GPs, to hamstring the university's medical faculty, to contaminate Vienna with venereal disease...

CYPRIAN: Now, now, blood under the bridge. Privy Counsellor Winkler casually mentioned to me only yesterday –

OSKAR quickly enters from the ward.

OSKAR: Father, if you want to speak to her, then –

BERNHARDI: Sorry, Cyprian – could you wait five minutes?

He exits to the ward.

OSKAR: (*To CYPRIAN.*) A decease, professor. Just a girl.

He follows BERNHARDI.

KURT: (*Casually.*) Sepsis. Abortion.

HOCHROITZPOINTNER: One for the slab tomorrow, Dr Adler.

CYPRIAN: (*In his monotone manner.*) When I was an assistant, I knew a rather shifty MD who told us to call him to every decease. Wanted to write a psychology of death, apparently. All very well but he didn't count on his own demise, did he? He was found cut to ribbons in some seedy beer-house on the wrong side of town. Very spurious. Married, with brood. By day, a doctor; by night, God-knows-what.

Enter PRIEST (a young man of twenty-eight; energetic, intelligent features).

ADLER: (*Assiduously.*) Hello, father.

PRIEST: Hello, gentlemen. I hope I'm not too late.

KURT: No, father. Professor Bernhardi's with the patient now. (*He introduces himself.*) Dr Kurt Pflugfelder, his assistant.

PRIEST: So it's not completely hopeless?

OSKAR comes out of the ward.

OSKAR: Good morning, father.

KURT: Oh, yes, father, *completely.*

OSKAR: (*To the PRIEST.*) Would you like to –?

PRIEST: I'll wait, perhaps, till the professor's finished with her?

HOCHROITZPOINTNER pushes a chair towards the PRIEST.

Thank you. (*He doesn't sit.*)

CYPRIAN: Some patients are beyond our help, father... Sometimes we, too, can only lend comfort.

KURT: And lies.

PRIEST: (*Sitting.*) That's rather unfeeling, doctor.

KURT: I'm sorry, father, I was only talking about doctors. Anyway, this is often the most difficult part of a doctor's job – and the most noble.

BERNHARDI appears at the door. The PRIEST stands. NURSE LUDMILLA enters after BERNHARDI.

BERNHARDI: (*Somewhat put out.*) Oh...father.

PRIEST: I can take over from you, professor. (*He holds out his hand.*) She's still conscious?

BERNHARDI: Yes. You could say she's more conscious than ever. (*More to the others.*) She's euphoric. (*As if explaining to the PRIEST.*) She's quite well, in a way.

PRIEST: Wonderful! Who knows? I know someone who was ready for death a few months ago, I gave him the last rites. I saw him on the street yesterday, a healthy man!

ADLER: And it might have been you who gave him back his strength for life, father.

BERNHARDI: But the priest has missed my point, doctor. (*To the PRIEST.*) I meant the patient's ignorant of her condition. She thinks she's recovered, but she hasn't.

PRIEST: I see.

BERNHARDI: I worry, father, that the sight of you –

PRIEST: (*Very mildly.*) Don't be afraid for her. I'm not here to pronounce a death sentence.

BERNHARDI: Of course not, all the same –

PRIEST: If the patient could be readied.

Unnoticed by BERNHARDI, on an almost indiscernible wink from the PRIEST, NURSE LUDMILLA exits to the ward.

BERNHARDI: But this isn't going to help. The last thing she expects is you. As I said, she's unaware of the reality. And she's happy. She thinks her loved-ones are on their way; she thinks she's about to resume her life. Father, I don't think it'd be a good thing – I'd almost venture to say it'd be quite an un-Godly thing – if you were to shake her out of her delusion.

PRIEST: (*After hesitating briefly; more firmly.*) Is there the possibility that my presence…that I might somehow affect the course of the illness in a negative –

BERNHARDI: (*Interrupting quickly.*) You *might* hasten the end, only by minutes, probably, but still –

PRIEST: (*More animatedly.*) I ask again: could your patient recover? Would my presence pose any danger in this respect? If so, I'll leave immediately, of course.

ADLER nods approvingly.

BERNHARDI: There's no doubt about it: she's dying.

PRIEST: Then, professor, I don't see why –

BERNHARDI: Forgive me, father, but I'm here in my capacity as a doctor. One of my responsibilities, when everything else is beyond me, is to help my patients to die happily – at least as much as I can.

CYPRIAN shows slight impatience and disapproval.

PRIEST: I think we take 'die happily' to mean different things. I've already heard from your nurse that this patient needs absolution more than many others.

BERNHARDI: (*With his ironic smile.*) We're all sinners, aren't we?

PRIEST: This isn't the time or place, professor. Her end's near; somewhere at the bottom of her soul, in a place only God can see, she's longing to finally confess her sins. You can't know otherwise.

BERNHARDI: Do I really need to repeat myself, father? – she doesn't know she's dying. She's not contrite, she's happy.

PRIEST: All the more reason for me not to budge till I've administered the consolations of our holy religion. I'd carry a heavy blame otherwise.

BERNHARDI: God and any earthly judge will relieve you from that.

He responds to a movement from the PRIEST.

Yes, father. I'm a doctor. And I can't let you go to my patient.

PRIEST: I was called. So I –

BERNHARDI: *I* didn't ask anyone to call you. Her welfare is entrusted to me till the end. And, unfortunately, as a doctor, I have to forbid you from walking through that door.

PRIEST: (*Stepping forward.*) Forbid me?

BERNHARDI: (*Lightly touching his shoulder.*) Yes, father.

NURSE LUDMILLA hurries in from the ward.

NURSE LUDMILLA: Father!

BERNHARDI: Nurse Ludmilla? You went to her –?

NURSE LUDMILLA: (*To PRIEST.*) It's too late.

KURT exits into the ward quickly.

BERNHARDI: (*To NURSE LUDMILLA.*) Did you tell the patient a priest was here?

NURSE LUDMILLA: Yes, professor.

BERNHARDI: I see. Don't panic. Answer me. Did she say anything? Well?

NURSE LUDMILLA: She said –

BERNHARDI: Speak.

NURSE LUDMILLA: She was distressed.

BERNHARDI: (*Not angrily.*) What did she say, exactly?

NURSE LUDMILLA: 'Am I really going to die?'

KURT enters from the ward.

KURT: It's over.

Short pause.

BERNHARDI: Don't be alarmed, father. It's not your fault. You wanted to do your duty, I wanted to do mine. I'm sorry enough I didn't succeed.

PRIEST: You're not in a position to pardon me, professor. That miserable thing has died a sinner, without the consolations of religion. And it's your fault.

BERNHARDI: I take the blame.

PRIEST: It remains to be seen whether you'll be able to do that. Goodbye.

He leaves. The others remain, uneasy and embarrassed. BERNHARDI looks at them one by one.

BERNHARDI: Well now, Dr Adler: autopsy at eight.

CYPRIAN: (*To BERNHARDI, sotto voce.*) That wasn't right.

BERNHARDI: Why not?

CYPRIAN: One case? You think you can change things?

BERNHARDI: *Things?* What are you talking about, Cyprian? As if that were my intention.

ADLER: It would be disingenuous of me, professor, if I didn't say here that I can't support you, formally, over this matter.

BERNHARDI: It would be disingenuous of me, Dr Adler, if I didn't say I guessed as much.

CYPRIAN and ADLER exit. OSKAR bites his lip.

Well, son, hopefully it won't wreck *your* career.

OSKAR: Father!

BERNHARDI: (*Taking his head, tenderly.*) I'm sorry, I didn't mean that.

NURSE LUDMILLA: Professor, I thought –

BERNHARDI: What, exactly? It doesn't matter, it's over.

NURSE LUDMILLA: But we always… And – (*She points at HOCHROITZPOINTNER.*) Mr Hoch –

HOCHROITZPOINTNER: Yes – and of course I didn't stop her, Professor Bernhardi.

BERNHARDI: No, Mr Hochroitzpointner. You take a place in the church pew, I suppose?

HOCHROITZPOINTNER: We live in a Christian state, professor.

BERNHARDI: Yes. (*He stares at him for a long time.*) God forgive you; you know what you bloody well do.

He, KURT and OSKAR exit. NURSE LUDMILLA is struggling to hold back tears.

HOCHROITZPOINTNER: Why did you try to make an excuse? You did your duty, simple as that. What's wrong with you, girl, pull yourself together.

NURSE LUDMILLA: (*Sobbing.*) But the Director, he was so cross!

HOCHROITZPOINTNER: Who cares? Doesn't matter. Director!? Not for much longer. The man just dug his own grave.

End of Act One.

Act Two

PROFESSOR BERNHARDI's surgery. One door leads to the hall, another to an adjacent room. A medicine cupboard; bookshelves; stove with a bust of Aesculapius, Greco-Roman god of medicine; desk; small table; sofa; chairs; photographs of scholars. OSKAR is welcoming PROFESSOR FILITZ (Professor of Gynaecology; forty; handsome, blond; pince-nez).

OSKAR: Professor Filitz…

FILITZ: Good morning, Oskar. I was just accosted on the doorstep by a very hungry-looking GP.

OSKAR: Yes, Dr Feuermann, he's an old friend of mine.

FILITZ: (*Affably.*) Polished off a teacher's wife in Oberhollabrun: bled to death after delivery.

OSKAR: There's to be a hearing. Did he ask for your help?

FILITZ: He did.

OSKAR: It was a series of unlucky coincidences…

FILITZ: Coincidences wouldn't happen if young people weren't tearing in practice before they're ready. Man had the gall to say if he were a professor he'd be off the hook, because *then* the authorities would put it down to God! Obviously another whippersnapper who thinks he owes it to his scientific dignity to act the atheist. Listen up, Oskar, without faith, science is an uncertain thing. No faith? No moral foundation, no ethos.

OSKAR: He's really very capable.

FILITZ: Don't you worry about your Feuerstein friend. I'll find a way to help the poor bugger out of his mess.

OSKAR: Feuermann.

FILITZ: Hmn?

OSKAR: Not Feuerstein.

FILITZ: Yes. Papa around?

OSKAR: He's in Baden with Archduke Konstantin. I'm expecting him any minute.

FILITZ: I haven't got a lot of time. (*He looks at his watch.*) Be good enough to tell him – you'll be interested in this yourself – tell him that Princess Stixenstein didn't receive my wife this morning.

OSKAR: (*Not quite comprehending.*) Oh. She was busy?

FILITZ: In her capacity as President of the Ball Committee, my wife was invited to see Princess Stixenstein – ball patroness and wife of the President of our Board – at eleven sharp.

He fixes him with his gaze, as is his wont. OSKAR is embarrassed.

What is it you don't understand, Oskar?

The HOUSEKEEPER enters with a card. OSKAR looks at it.

Don't let me keep you.

OSKAR: Dr Löwenstein. (*To the HOUSEKEEPER.*) Show him in.

The HOUSEKEEPER exits.

FILITZ: I have to go anyway.

Enter DR LÖWENSTEIN (Lecturer in Paediatrics; forty-ish; medium height, small eyes, sloping left shoulder; spectacles; hurried, restless and confrontational, with a habit of running his fingers through his hair).

LÖWENSTEIN: Oskar, hello – ah, Professor Filitz, don't leave. You'll want to hear this. (*To OSKAR*.) Read.

He hands him a letter. OSKAR reads through it quickly.

Sorry, Filitz, but Oskar should read it first, as Vice-President of the Ball Committee. Princess Stixenstein. Her notice.

OSKAR: (*Handing the letter to FILITZ*.) Without saying why?

FILITZ: Blindingly obvious, I think.

OSKAR: It's…it's become public, then? In a week?

LÖWENSTEIN: The second I heard about it, Oskar, I said to myself, 'Fish to their net…'

FILITZ: Stop exaggerating, Dr Löwenstein. The plain and simple fact is – actually, I'd prefer to say what I think to my friend Bernhardi in person.

OSKAR: It goes without saying, professor, that I'm on Father's side completely.

FILITZ: Of course, that's your duty.

OSKAR: And my conviction, professor.

LÖWENSTEIN: And mine, Filitz. I emphatically believe a spiteful something has been fabricated out of an innocent nothing. To be explicit: there'd be no such fabrication if Bernhardi didn't happen to be a Jew.

FILITZ: Here we go again, your *idée fixe*. I'm an anti-Semite, I suppose? Even though I've always had at least one Jewish assistant? There's no anti-Semitism towards decent Jews.

LÖWENSTEIN: Oh, really? – I don't see it like that –

FILITZ: If a Christian had done it we'd still be having this conversation.

LÖWENSTEIN: Fine. Possibly. But that Christian would have thousands of allies – hundreds of thousands. Today they're mute. Too busy sharpening their claws.

FILITZ: Who do you mean?

LÖWENSTEIN: The German Nationalists, and of course the Jews – I mean a certain type who'd do anything to stay in favour with the great and good.

FILITZ: Honestly, Löwenstein, all this persecution talk is maniacal. People are different, it's a pity they sometimes clash, but it's made a hundred times worse by men like you, sniffing out anti-Semitism left, right and centre. Things would be better if –

BERNHARDI enters. He seems in a good mood, with his ironic smile. Greetings and handshakes.

BERNHARDI: Gentlemen! What's up? Did they burn us down? Or did someone bequeath us a million?

OSKAR: (*Handing him the letter.*) The Princess has resigned as patroness of the ball.

BERNHARDI: (*Skimming the letter.*) Lose one princess, find another. (*Jokingly.*) Or are you joining her band and quitting as Vice-President, Oskar?

OSKAR: (*Somewhat offended.*) Father –

LÖWENSTEIN: Bernhardi, your son's just solemnly said he stands shoulder to shoulder with you.

BERNHARDI: (*Tenderly stroking OSKAR's hair.*) Yes. No offence meant, Oskar. You know that, Löwenstein.

OSKAR: I'll leave you to it. (*He smiles.*) We've got a Ball Committee meeting at six. Goodbye, Professor Filitz. Goodbye, Dr Löwenstein.

They shake hands. OSKAR exits.

BERNHARDI: Now, Filitz: you look as if our house really *is* a pile of ashes.

FILITZ: This morning, Princess Stixenstein refused to see my wife.

BERNHARDI: Oh. And?

FILITZ: She's walked out as patroness – and she refused to admit my wife.

BERNHARDI: Yes. And?

FILITZ: Don't be simple, Bernhardi. You know perfectly well that as trivial as it may be in itself, it's extremely telling. A certain matter is being received in a certain manner in high-ranking circles.

BERNHARDI: (*Very cheerfully.*) I've just got back from the highest. Archduke Konstantin. Knows the whole story – and he received it in a manner radically different from HH Princess Stixenstein.

FILITZ: The Archduke, Bernhardi? It's a sport: hunting, fishing, progressive thinking.

BERNHARDI: Still –

FILITZ: Anyway I don't give a turnip what Archduke Konstantin thinks. Though I might as well say that where your actions and behaviour in this are concerned, I disagree with him.

BERNHARDI: Did your wife send you to give me a telling off?

FILITZ: (*Furiously.*) I'd never *dream* of… I'm here to ask what you're planning to do to make amends to her for the snub.

BERNHARDI: (*Truly surprised.*) But…you don't seriously mean –

CYPRIAN enters.

CYPRIAN: Gentlemen, hello. Sorry to barge in –

He shakes everyone's hand.

BERNHARDI: Let me guess, a princess has left us patron-less?

CYPRIAN: The ball's the least of it…

FILITZ: (*Looking at his watch.*) Excuse me, Cyprian. Bernhardi, once again: what do you plan to do to make amends to my wife after Princess Stixenstein's snub?

LÖWENSTEIN looks at CYPRIAN.

BERNHARDI: (*Very calmly.*) My friend. Tell your lovely wife that I think her too clever to believe for a second that she'd be truly upset at being barred entry to the salon of her Most Transcendent Highness the Princess Goose.

FILITZ: There's nothing else to say after a remark like that. Goodbye, gentlemen.

He exits quickly.

CYPRIAN: You shouldn't have said that.

LÖWENSTEIN: Why not?

CYPRIAN: Aside from the fact that it was red rag to a bull, he's wrong. Princess Stixenstein's no goose. In fact, she's very smart.

BERNHARDI: Babette Stixenstein, smart?

LÖWENSTEIN: Try pig-headed, bitchy, bigoted…

BERNHARDI paces.

CYPRIAN: What does it matter? Forget her – what about her husband? He'll have his own ideas… Perhaps the Board will resign as one.

LÖWENSTEIN: No! – that would be beyond the pale.

BERNHARDI: (*Stopping in front of CYPRIAN.*) Not possible. It's made up of Stixenstein, the Archduke, Bishop Liebenberg, Veith, and our friend Winkler from the Ministry. Apart from Stixenstein, I guarantee –

CYPRIAN: I wouldn't guarantee anything, if I were you.

BERNHARDI: I was called to Archduke Konstantin's an hour ago – the man's fit as a flea, it was a stunt so we could have a chat.

LÖWENSTEIN: And?

BERNHARDI: (*Somewhat flattered, smiling.*) He said a couple of hundred years ago, I'd have been burnt at the stake.

CYPRIAN: Oh, very encouraging.

BERNHARDI: He also said, 'And I'd be up there with you'.

LÖWENSTEIN: Ha!

CYPRIAN: Even though he goes to Mass and votes in the Upper House against anything that looks like reform – ?

BERNHARDI: Well, there *are* official obligations for a crown prince.

LÖWENSTEIN: Now, what about the Bishop?

BERNHARDI: The Archduke told me something the Bishop said, actually: 'I like the man.'

LÖWENSTEIN: You like the Bishop?

BERNHARDI: The Bishop likes me.

LÖWENSTEIN: So: the Archduke, the Bishop... Who's left? Winkler from the Ministry.

BERNHARDI: He won't sell us down the river.

CYPRIAN: Back to the Bishop, if I may – you didn't get the full quote. He said, 'I like Bernhardi,' then added, 'though he's going to regret this'.

LÖWENSTEIN: Who told you that?

CYPRIAN: Winkler. In his office, an hour ago. And he *will* sell you down the river if the rest have done the same thing.

BERNHARDI: Not if he's the man we take him for.

LÖWENSTEIN: He's not a man, he's a civil servant.

CYPRIAN: What good would it do him to take your side?

BERNHARDI: Enough of this, it isn't about *me.*

CYPRIAN: Right, it's about the Institute.

LÖWENSTEIN: So we lose them! It's not as if the Archduke and Bishop have opened their purses over the years.

CYPRIAN: Maybe not, but I can name you a dozen Jews who donate to us for two reasons: A – there's an archduke on the Board; B – a bishop. And if the money dries up, so do we.

BERNHARDI: You're exaggerating. This is all happening because I did my duty as a doctor.

LÖWENSTEIN: Scandalous! Let the Institute collapse – we'll found another one, a better one, without Filitz and Ebenwald and the rest. I warned you about this lot, Bernhardi – you've always been too easy to fleece.

CYPRIAN: (*Having tried in vain to pacify him.*) Shut up, Löwenstein. The Institute's still here. And, for now, we have a Board. And Privy Counsellor Winkler, who likes you, thinks there might yet be a way to stop this thing in its tracks.

BERNHARDI: Oh?

LÖWENSTEIN: I suppose it's an apology or something unctuous like that? Huh! It *is*!

CYPRIAN: No one's suggesting he wears sackcloth and ashes at the church door. No one's suggesting a retraction. (*To BERNHARDI.*) A simple expression of regret –

BERNHARDI: But I don't regret anything.

LÖWENSTEIN: The opposite.

CYPRIAN: Surely you could explain, without compromising yourself, that it was never your intention to cause any religious offence.

BERNHARDI: But people know that.

CYPRIAN: Oh, you're always talking as if everyone is good! Of course people know it – the people who want your neck in a noose know it better than anyone! Bernhardi, the signs are there: they're planning to depict you as an evil-doer; as a man who's cocked a snook at the Church –

BERNHARDI: But – !

CYPRIAN: The accusation's coming: you should have guarded yourself against this indiscretion, you especially, as you don't have the *sine qua non* to understand the inner meaning of the Catholic sacraments.

BERNHARDI: Now –

CYPRIAN: Oh look, I've heard it all. From 'good' people, 'enlightened' people. Forget them, worry about the others.

LÖWENSTEIN: The mob, you mean?

CYPRIAN: I'm mighty sick of your high-minded indignation, Löwenstein. Yes, the mob: it exists. (*To BERNHARDI.*) Fine, you could never engage with it; but you won't change people with obstinacy. Do what you can to calm things down, please. A statement: no offence intended. You can make it tomorrow, when we meet to discuss Professor Tugendvetter's successor.

BERNHARDI: Yes, *that's* what we should be talking about, not this damn –

CYPRIAN: I agree! I'm not asking you to abandon your principles. A simple statement.

BERNHARDI: And you think –

LÖWENSTEIN: Bernhardi, no! Do it, and I'll pick up the torch, as if *I'd* stopped the priest–

CYPRIAN: The man's a rabble-rouser, Bernhardi...

BERNHARDI paces.

...what if this were Oskar's future on the line? Would you worry about pride then? Think how hard you've had to defend the Institute. Don't lose control now. Why sap yourself dry in a pointless fracas? You're a doctor. What's more important: saving a human life, or a placard?

LÖWENSTEIN: Oh, how fallacious!

CYPRIAN: The Institute's at a crossroads. It's down to you, Bernhardi. Listen. If we turn the right way, our future *is* guaranteed. A brilliant future.

BERNHARDI stops pacing, surprised.

I spoke to Minister Flint.

BERNHARDI: About this?

CYPRIAN: No, we deliberately skirted it. He really has changed his mind about us. And he's sorry he fell out with you.

LÖWENSTEIN: Flint would sell his grandmother.

CYPRIAN: Yes, he warms to his themes – but why not fan them, if it's in our interest? He longs for a reconciliation. And he wants to put the Institute right in the middle of new plans to reform medical education and public health in Austria.

BERNHARDI: Ten years ago because we treated every kind of illness, we were responsible for every outbreak of illness; we were a bunch of pushy young upstarts; a moral threat to Vienna. I know him too well.

CYPRIAN: He's older and wiser. The Minister's our friend. The Institute, Bernhardi. Our Institute.

Short pause.

BERNHARDI: Dinner. Half-past nine. I'll bring an outline.

LÖWENSTEIN: Bernhardi!

BERNHARDI: No…it's true…I don't want to play the hero at any cost. I think I already have a reputation as a man who gets his way when it's *really* necessary. So… perhaps there is a way…to come up with something.

CYPRIAN: Make it typically ironic, if you like. A wry smile isn't going to reach the ears of Princess Stixenstein, is it?

LÖWENSTEIN: What kind of men are you?

CYPRIAN: Shut up, Löwenstein. You're just a spectator with nothing to lose.

LÖWENSTEIN: No. I stand alone.

CYPRIAN: (*To BERNHARDI.*) Nine-thirty at the Riedhof, with a draft.

BERNHARDI: One that won't insult even *your* religious feelings, Löwenstein.

LÖWENSTEIN: Oh, very rich.

BERNHARDI shakes hands with them and they exit. He paces, looks at the clock, shakes his head, takes out his notebook, looks something up, then pockets it again as if to say, 'that can wait'. He sits, takes a sheet of paper and begins to write. He is serious at first, and then the customary smile crosses his lips. The HOUSEKEEPER enters and hands him a card. He hesitates a moment.

BERNHARDI: Show him in.

The HOUSEKEEPER exits. EBENWALD appears at the door.

EBENWALD: Bernhardi...

BERNHARDI: (*Extending a hand.*) Ebenwald. To what do I owe the pleasure?

EBENWALD: I'll get straight to the point, if you don't mind.

BERNHARDI: Not at all.

He invites him to sit.

EBENWALD: I have to tell you there's movement against you, and therefore, our Institute.

BERNHARDI: The rumour the Board's about to resign *en masse*? Storm in a teacup.

EBENWALD: The Board's about to resign? First I've heard of it. Hmn. Shall I compound this bleak news? There's going to be a question asked about you in Parliament.

BERNHARDI: Oh! Well, that won't happen.

EBENWALD: Really? I take it you have a trick to stop the scandal on the street? But how can you stop a parliamentary question?

BERNHARDI: Wait and see.

EBENWALD: That's one option. As Vice-Director, my recommendation is that a method be found to prevent this tedious matter from ever reaching the House.

BERNHARDI: Not so straightforward, is it, if it's being pressed by zealous politicians? If they need their explanation in the name of the religion I've offended, nothing on earth will stop them.

EBENWALD: Well... If they could just be made to understand there was *no* offence, or no *large* offence. If they could just see there's no – how should I put it? – no deliberate anti-Catholic bias –

BERNHARDI: Why spell it out to them?

EBENWALD: I'm not suggesting that. I'm suggesting *proof.*

BERNHARDI: Ah, the plot thickens. What would such proof look like?

EBENWALD: A specific case. From which the conclusion – no anti-Catholic bias – could be drawn without doubt.

BERNHARDI: (*Impatiently.*) But we'd have to *build* such a case!

EBENWALD: Already exists.

BERNHARDI: What are you talking about?

EBENWALD: Tomorrow, we decide on Professor Tugendvetter's successor.

BERNHARDI: Ah!

EBENWALD: (*Coolly.*) Quite. There are two candidates.

BERNHARDI: (*Very firmly.*) One who deserves the job, one who doesn't.

EBENWALD: Dermatology and Syphilis isn't really your field, Bernhardi, and –

BERNHARDI: It's risible to mention the two men in the same breath, and you know it. Dr Hell's published one or two tolerable articles (in priceless German); Dr Wenger's works are revelatory.

EBENWALD: (*Very calmly.*) Don't agree. And Dr Wenger's not popular. Even his friends don't like him.

BERNHARDI: (*Increasingly impatient.*) This is neither here nor there, *I* don't decide, we as a committee do.

EBENWALD: You *do* decide in the case of an equal vote. For Dr Wenger: Cyprian, Löwenstein, Adler, that old revolutionary Pflugfelder –

BERNHARDI: And Tugendvetter.

EBENWALD: You don't believe that.

BERNHARDI: What, has he already promised you his vote?

EBENWALD: That wouldn't be proof. You know as well as I he won't give his vote to Wenger. His own assistant! If that doesn't say something ...

BERHARDI: Tugendvetter should be more appreciative. His recent articles carry his name and Wenger's research.

EBENWALD: Perhaps you should say that to Professor Tugendvetter's face?

BERNHARDI: Professor, it's always been my custom to tell people what I think of them in person. Stop.

Stop being dishonest. You're campaigning for Dr Hell because – because he's not a Jew.

EBENWALD: (*Very calmly.*) I've the right to respond, professor, that you're campaigning for Dr Wenger because –

BERNHARDI: It's obviously slipped your mind I voted for *you* three years ago, Ebenwald?

EBENWALD: You swallowed hard, though, hmn? And I'd have to do the same for Wenger. I won't. I'd regret it. Even if I had a higher opinion of him, the fact is, in institutions in the public eye, things don't boil down to talent alone –

BERNHARDI: But also to *character*.

EBENWALD: I was going to say *climate*, actually – and we're back to where we started. Appalling, I know, that questions of personnel in Austria are so political, but what can we do? If Dr Hell were a dimwit I wouldn't vote for him, or ask it of you. But he's as talented as Wenger. If in addition we can get rid of the…putrid smell of…a certain…mess of your doing…can't guarantee it, of course…it's just an idea that occurred to me…

BERNHARDI: To you?

EBENWALD: But one worth trying. False pride, Bernhardi. Think about it, and let's talk again before the committee meeting. All of this is confidential, of course.

BERNHARDI: Forget discretion, professor. Tell the men who sent you –

EBENWALD: How *dare* –

BERNHARDI: – tell them I don't accept deals –

EBENWALD: I *won't* take your order, I'm here unofficially, I want that noted! No one's sent me! And it's not to save my skin – I don't have to answer for your conduct towards that priest. It's for the Institute. And you. I came as a friend.

BERNHARDI: You leave an enemy. I'd prefer that, at least it's honest.

EBENWALD: You've made your choice. Goodbye.

BERNHARDI: Goodbye.

He accompanies EBENWALD to the door, EBENWALD exits. BERNHARDI is alone. He paces, then grabs the paper he was writing on earlier. He reads it through and tears it up. He looks at his watch and settles himself. The HOUSEKEEPER enters with a card.

Minister Flint? Here?

HOUSEKEEPER: Yes, sir.

BERNHARDI: Well. You'd better show him in.

Enter FLINT (the Minister for Education and Cultural Affairs; fifties; tall, thin; short hair, neat side-burns; the conscious mask of a diplomat; very affable, often genuinely warm).

Excellency? *(He smiles ironically.)*

FLINT: *(Shaking his hand.)* It's been a while, Bernhardi.

BERNHARDI: Some do or other.

FLINT: In private, I mean.

BERNHARDI: Yes, true. Please, sit down.

FLINT: Thank you.

He sits. BERNHARDI follows suit.

(Casually.) Surprised?

BERNHARDI: Pleasantly. I can congratulate you on your new position. Quite an honour.

65

FLINT: You know I don't see it like that. Still, thank you. Course it's not why I'm here…

BERNHARDI: No.

FLINT: Bernhardi.

BERNHARDI: Excellency?

FLINT: I'm looking for people.

BERNHARDI: People?

FLINT: And I'm wondering if I can count on you. I only have my portfolio a few years, don't want to be slack, must carry out many reforms…in medical education, public health…things I've been passionate about since I was a young man, as you know. Now, I've got civil servants, and we have able civil servants in Austria – some are even at the Ministry – but their world view is rather basic. I want volunteers. Autonomous, unbiased…*people.*

Slight pause.

BERNHARDI: Could you be more precise?

FLINT: Hmn. Sharp as ever. Was prepared for it. It's why I have particular faith in you. We've had our differences –

BERNHARDI: (*Seriously.*) That's understating it, Flint. There was a time when we were best friends.

FLINT: (*Sincerely.*) We drifted apart. It happens. Circumstances. Laws of maturity. Why bear a grudge?

BERNHARDI: I've got a very good memory.

FLINT: Don't muddy present waters. Bury the hatchet. New day dawns.

BERNHARDI: Not so simple. Not that those three sentences *were* –

FLINT: Bernhardi, stop being obstreperous, what's important is today –

BERNHARDI: (*Standing.*) No, Flint. I won't forget your dirty tactics. You did everything you could to bring my Institute into disrepute. You persecuted us.

FLINT: Dear Bernhardi, I *did* think the place a little unsavoury; but over time we've come to appreciate the scientific and humanitarian good you've done. Believe me, the Institute has no better friend... It wasn't personal... I had certain convictions, and if there's one thing I *can* say, it's that I've never compromised on those.

BERNHARDI: Really?

FLINT: (*A little uncertainly.*) Made mistakes, of course, haven't we all? Convictions, though, are convictions.

BERNHARDI: You acted against yours once. And someone died.

FLINT: Steady on.

BERNHARDI: (*Pacing, spurred on.*) We were assistants. There was a patient, a junior official, I even remember his name, Engelbert Wagner. Our boss had made the wrong diagnosis – we all had. At the autopsy, we found he could have been saved with another treatment. Syphilis case, remember? And as we stood there, realisation dawning, you whispered to me, 'I knew it'. You made the correct diagnosis.

FLINT: The only one who did.

BERNHARDI: But you didn't speak up while he was alive! Why? Conviction?

FLINT: Damn you've got a good memory. Yes, I kept my trap shut. Because our chief was a prickly so-and-so who couldn't stand it when assistants showed him up. You accuse me, perhaps reasonably, of letting a man die. You're wrong about the reasons. One sacrifice, made in favour of the hundreds of other lives I'd subsequently save. I needed all the help I could get – I was on the brink of securing the professorship in Prague.

BERNHARDI: You think you'd have been out on your ear if –?

FLINT: More than likely. You overrate men, Bernhardi. Wouldn't have cost me my career, but it would have set me back – and I wanted to get on with it. No regrets. A *single* case. In the wider sense, immaterial. Nothing to do with the heart of one's beliefs. Fascinating you've hoisted poor Engelbert out of his box. You're what they call decent. Sentimental. But you're not more adept than I of achieving good for the greater whole. You don't have an eye for what's *really* important: to serve the inherent idea of your life. To cling like a limpet to the right thing in a petty singular case...it's missing the point. It does lack *scale*. So narrow-minded. Dogmatic. Immoral, frankly.

BERNHARDI: Something particular in mind, Flint?

FLINT: Mmn, floated into my field of vision as I was wittering on.

BERNHARDI: The nub of the matter, at last!

FLINT: Not at all. Since you're broaching the subject... In that cuddly but sometimes unfortunate manner of yours, you failed, in the heat of the moment, to look beyond the ward. Teeny-tiny fact: your ward is in a Christian state. Something funny?

BERNHARDI: I've just remembered something else, you'll love this one. An article you wanted to write once. Catchy title: 'Churches or Hospitals?' Thesis: more hospitals, fewer churches.

FLINT: There were piles of articles I *wanted* to write. Hospitals, churches, they can co-exist happily, I know that now. Half the illnesses that still baffle we scientists are taken care of in church. Anyway, the tide's turning against you. I honestly wish for your sake, and the Institute's, that we turn it back.

BERNHARDI: I wish that as well, Flint.

FLINT: You do?

BERNHARDI: Yes! – I've more important things to do with my time. I even had a word with Cyprian and Löwenstein about making a statement…so the 'offended' parties will be satisfied.

FLINT: Really? Goodie. Though given the latest details perhaps not quite enough.

BERNHARDI: Latest –?

FLINT: If – you wouldn't be compromising yourself, I think – especially since, as far as I know, the police aren't involved, yet – if perhaps you could visit the priest? – that'd create a first-rate impression. You did, after all, obstruct him, by force, as it were –

BERNHARDI: Force?

FLINT: Clearly too Herculean a word. Still, you did…so one hears…stand in front of the door, and…shove him, with some ferocity.

BERNHARDI: That is a lie.

FLINT: You didn't shove him?

BERNHARDI: I hardly touched him! I know who's behind this, I *won't let* –

FLINT: Calm down, Bernhardi. You haven't been charged with anything. If you've decided to make a statement, easy enough to debunk the tittle-tattle at the same time –

BERNHARDI: Flint. I'm sorry. You've misunderstood. I did have a statement in mind, but I can't make it now. Things have changed. It's impossible.

FLINT: What's changed?

BERNHARDI: (*Smiling.*) Did you really come here to pull me out of a tight spot?

FLINT: I wouldn't feel guilty about letting you face the music, Bernhardi. You behaved incorrectly towards the priest. But I care about the Institute – and about you.

BERNHARDI: But what you *really* want is to be spared the question in Parliament, no?

FLINT: Yes.

BERNHARDI: You won't believe it, Excellency! I could have done it for you! Twenty minutes ago!

FLINT: Hmn?

BERNHARDI: The meeting about Professor Tugendvetter's successor is tomorrow. If I'd made a promise to give my deciding vote to Dr Hell, not Dr Wenger, the question would have been stopped!

FLINT: A promise? To – ?

BERNHARDI: Professor Ebenwald.

FLINT: You're telling me you think Ebenwald somehow –

BERNHARDI: Yes, I think he had the power to see a deal through – though he denied it when I challenged him.

FLINT: (*Pacing.*) Ebenwald's very thick with his cousin in the House. Ottokar's a leading clerical, he definitely has the clout to stop a question. Well! Hanky-panky! What did you say?

BERNHARDI: Flint!

FLINT: You think Wenger's the better doctor?

BERNHARDI: Hell's an ass. Even if they were equally
distinguished, Ebenwald's manœuvre would have made
it impossible for me to vote for anyone but Wenger.

FLINT: Yes – not terribly bright of your Vice-Director.

BERNHARDI: You're pretty bloody indulgent.

FLINT: Bernhardi, politics –

BERNHARDI: I don't care about politics.

FLINT: Politics concerns everybody.

BERNHARDI: (*Warmly.*) Flint. I know you're a politician
now, but deep down, you're a man of science, truth.
As you said, it's about seeing what's important. What's
important here is that the most competent man gets
to contribute to science. Not that some question in
Parliament be stopped to save your hide or mine.
Honestly, a reasonable *answer* to the thing might be
found, after all!

FLINT: Hmn. I can hear it.

BERNHARDI: I'm sure.

FLINT: Bernhardi, be a sport, jot everything down? A
letter, with the ins and outs of the whole thing, the
incontrovertible truth. So that were I required to, you
know, answer, I'd have it in black and white. Might
not be necessary to read it out. If the question's asked,
I'll be epigrammatic. If they press it, dah-dah. (*He
gestures, as if producing the letter.*) But they won't. They'll
intuit I've got something big up my sleeve. One or two
well-placed words and Parliament's putty in my hands.
You know, once you've got their ear, you're never
wholly wrong about anything. At the risk of sounding

conceited, I'm almost beginning to wish the buggers *would* ask the question –

BERNHARDI: Flint!

FLINT: – because I feel this case symbolises our entire political state. Always happens to me. It's why politics was my destiny. I see in everything a metaphor for something else. I could go general with this.

BERNHARDI: 'More Hospitals, Fewer Churches'?

FLINT: You joke, but I won't make a sport of something this momentous.

BERNHARDI: One would almost think you were on my side, Flint.

FLINT: I *wasn't,* I admit it, and I still don't think your behaviour towards the priest was correct. But this Ebenwald deal throws a whole new light on things. Now this can't get out, or they might change their minds about asking the question. Hush-hush till I lay the letter on the table of the House. (*He gestures without exaggeration.*)

BERNHARDI: Flint, I'm…delighted…but are you sure it's worth it? The party you'd have to oppose stops at nothing. Would you be able to govern without it?

FLINT: It would depend on the challenge.

BERNHARDI: But if the Ministry's more important to you –

FLINT: Than you?

BERNHARDI: – than the truth – then you shouldn't stand up for me.

FLINT: You? This isn't about you, it's about justice!

BERNHARDI: It's a trivial matter. Are you sure it's worth it?

FLINT: Trivial? Don't you see what's at stake here? Light over dark! Trite though that sounds.

BERNHARDI: But you don't know you're going to win, not in this society. Your whole ministership –

FLINT: Let that be my problem. Whatever happens, what could be more glorious than to die fighting for justice? For the benefit of a man who, might as well admit it, was my enemy an hour ago.

BERNHARDI: I wasn't your enemy. And if I wronged you, I'm sorry. But let me say this, Flint: if everything comes crashing down, I won't feel any guilt. You know the truth. I'm not going to admire you for doing your duty.

FLINT: Nor should you, Bernhardi. When can you get the letter to me?

BERNHARDI: By morning?

FLINT shakes his hand.

FLINT: (*Lightly.*) I came here looking for a human being. I found him. Goodbye!

BERNHARDI: Goodbye, Flint! (*He hesitates.*) Thank you.

FLINT: Oh, no, no, never. Our mutual respect is built on firmer foundations than that.

He exits. BERNHARDI remains, reflecting.

BERNHARDI: We'll see, won't we?

End of Act Two.

Act Three

The conference room at the Elisabeth Institute. Evening. Long green table; cupboards; photographs of famous doctors; chandelier; portrait of the late Empress Elisabeth. HOCHROITZPOINTNER is copying into a large minute book. Enter DR SCHREIMANN (Lecturer in Throat Disease; tall, bald, swarthy, military moustache, duelling scar; spectacles; deep, upright and consciously Germanic; occasional Jewish vocal inflection.).

HOCHROITZPOINTNER: (*Jumping up.*) Hello, Dr Schreimann.

SCHREIMANN: Mr Hochroitzpointner. Recovered from the ball?

HOCHROITZPOINTNER: Not really, my head didn't make the pillow. Wasn't worth it. I danced till seven, was on Professor Bernhardi's ward by eight, surgery at ten, at twelve –

SCHREIMANN: (*Interrupting, sitting.*) I get it – you're in every nook and cranny. What are you doing?

HOCHROITZPOINTNER: Making a fair copy of the last meeting's minutes.

SCHREIMANN: How diligent. Hope you can read my scrawl. (*He reads over HOCHROITZPOINTNER's shoulder.*) 'Vote...four for the Associate Professor at the University of Graz, Dr Hell; four for Dr S. Wenger –' *Samuel,* Dr *Samuel* Wenger.

HOCHROITZPOINTNER: Oh...but that's not in the notes –

SCHREIMANN: Mystery as to why. My grandfather was Samuel, he always wrote his name in full. My name is Siegfried, I do the same.

HOCHROITZPOINTNER: (*Stupidly.*) Yes.

SCHREIMANN: (*Continuing.*) 'Professor Bernhardi made use of his statutory right in the case of an equal vote and decided for Dr Samuel Wenger, who is duly elected Head of Dermatology and Syphilis.'

Short pause.

Happy with your new chief?

HOCHROITZPOINTNER: (*Involuntarily bowing his head.*) Of course.

SCHREIMANN: (*Laughing, putting his hand on his shoulder.*) Stop being so deferential, Hochroitzpointner – you're not my assistant anymore.

HOCHROITZPOINTNER: Unfortunately, Dr Schreimann. Happy days.

SCHREIMANN: Mmn. Now when are you actually going to take your final *viva voce*?

EBENWALD enters.

EBENWALD: I'd like to know the same thing.

HOCHROITZPOINTNER: Hello, professor.

EBENWALD: Schreimann.

SCHREIMANN: Ebenwald.

EBENWALD: Hochroitzpointner – have some time off: take wing: swot. Do you understand what I'm saying? Then you can finish. What are you doing in here anyway?

SCHREIMANN: He's making a fair copy of the minutes for me. Isn't it sweet?

EBENWALD: Where would the Institute be without our student? Where would a *ball* be without him? You danced the night away last night, I hear?

HOCHROITZPOINTNER: (*Stupidly.*) Yes. And the morning.

SCHREIMANN: Didn't even find his pillow.

EBENWALD: Young ones, young ones. Have fun?

HOCHROITZPOINTNER: Yes, it was packed to the rafters. Lively as you like.

EBENWALD: Oh, it was hot, white-hot. You, young man, were dancing on a volcano!

HOCHROITZPOINTNER: I *did* sweat quite a lot, professor.

EBENWALD: (*Laughing.*) Ha! Right: take some time off: swot: sit the damn exam. And no more waltzing on volcanoes – even extinct ones. Bye!

He shakes his hand. SCHREIMANN does the same. HOCHROITZPOINTNER exits.

Minister Flint was there!

SCHREIMANN: And had Bernhardi's ear for half an hour.

EBENWALD: Very odd.

SCHREIMANN: At a *ball.*

EBENWALD: He must know the Board's resigned.

SCHREIMANN: As one of them was on the dancefloor, I suppose he does. That shifty Privy Counsellor of his, Winkler.

EBENWALD: Schemer.

SCHREIMANN: Anyway, it isn't official yet.

EBENWALD: As good as. Hence our meeting. So – (*He hesitates.*) can I count on you, Schreimann?

SCHREIMANN: (*Contentedly.*) Funny question. Yes –
when I agree with you. Happily, that's most of the time.

EBENWALD: On *some* issues, there might be a problem?

SCHREIMANN: I've already told you, Ebenwald, this
whole thing isn't about religion or denomination,
but tact. Even if I were a Nationalist Jew, I'd oppose
Bernhardi. I'd like to say, again, that I'm a German-
Austrian and Christian, just like you. Believe me, these
days it takes real guts for someone of my origin to say
that publicly. I'd have had an easier ride as a Zionist.

EBENWALD: You'd have been guaranteed a professorship
in Jerusalem.

SCHREIMANN: Pathetic, Ebenwald.

EBENWALD: Schreimann, you know my position
regarding you. But you have to admit these are very
confused times. In a very confusing country.

SCHREIMANN: Oh here we go again, those anonymous
letters you got.

EBENWALD: You're not still touchy over those? And they
weren't anonymous, they were signed. Old friends of
mine, bewildered that I'd allied myself to you. Don't
forget I was a dedicated German Nationalist as a
student. You know what that means. Tankard-thumping
fraternities, oak trees, no duelling for Jewish students or
students descended from –

SCHREIMANN: 'Because a Jew has no honour, a Jew
is subhuman, a Jew can't be insulted, so can't demand
satisfaction for an insult.' I got this duelling scar when I
was still a Jew.

EBENWALD: You see, a confused country. You take more
pride in your Jewish duelling scar than in all of your
Austro-Germany.

Enter PROFESSOR PFLUGFELDER (Professor of Optometry; KURT's father; sixty-five; spectacles; a scholar).

PFLUGFELDER: Evening, you two. You've heard the Board's resigned?

EBENWALD: Dear Professor Pflugfelder, it's why we're here; why the surprise?

PFLUGFELDER: Surprise? Me? Gave up surprise years ago. Can still feel disgust, though. This mud-flinging campaign against Bernhardi. Totally unjustified – don't you agree?

EBENWALD: I don't know anything about it.

PFLUGFELDER: Oh you *don't*, Ebenwald? So you don't know that Ottokar – you know, cousin of yours in the Lower House – is master mud-flinger?

EBENWALD: I beg your pardon?

PFLUGFELDER: I won't tar you with your cousin's brush. I'm sure you're right to deny any link beyond grand-parentage. Because *isn't* it all coming out? Sir Cousin began his career as a lion-like German Nationalist – now he's cat's-paw of the clerics. And *you're* not clerical, are you, Ebenwald? You're an old student of Germanity. Remind me of the German virtues again? Courage, faithfulness, loyalty. Forget one, did I? – never mind, that's enough for us to be getting on with – which is why I know you'll agree we give Bernhardi our full support tonight.

EBENWALD: For what? What's happened to *him*? The only thing that's happened is that the Board's resigned. So we should shut up shop, frankly, because soon we'll be stony-broke. Three cheers for the Director, whose tactlessness has landed us in penury.

PFLUGFELDER: I see. Never mind. A leopard can't

change his spots, can he? I'd still let you poke around my innards, doctor. What about you, Schreimann? Bit quiet. Also against Bernhardi? Also furious he asked a priest to let a sick child die in peace? Understandable. Still wet behind the ears, aren't they, *your* Christian feelings? Treat with care.

EBENWALD: (*Calmly.*) Ignore him, Schreimann.

SCHREIMANN: (*Perfectly calmly.*) As I said to my colleague, professor, my religious feelings weren't offended one jot. My good taste was. There's no place for politics on the ward.

PFLUGFELDER: Bernhardi acted *politically*?! Balls, you don't believe that –

FILITZ enters. General greetings.

FILITZ: Gentlemen. I'm following the Board: I'm going to resign.

EBENWALD: What?

PFLUGFELDER: You're –

FILITZ: What else can I do? If I'm not going to stick up for him, then –

EBENWALD: Filitz, I don't agree, there's another way. We can't turn our backs on the place, we have to make the Board withdraw its resignation.

FILITZ: Won't happen as long as Bernhardi's in charge.

SCHREIMANN: Precisely. As long as.

PFLUGFELDER: Oh, you're already thinking of *that* – ?

ADLER enters.

ADLER: Evening, all. Read the paper?

EBENWALD: Why?

ADLER: The question in Parliament.

SCHREIMANN: Over Bernhardi?

FILITZ: Happened already?

ADLER: *The Chronicle* has run a special evening edition.

EBENWALD: (*At the door, calling.*) You there, nurse! (*To ADLER.*) We haven't read it.

SCHREIMANN: Doctors, you see – don't have time to loll about in cafés all afternoon perusing the papers.

EBENWALD: (*To FILITZ.*) I wasn't expecting this till tomorrow. (*At the door, yelling.*) Nurse, please run and buy us a *Chronicle*, would you? Evening edition!

FILITZ: Get two!

SCHREIMANN: Six!

EBENWALD: (*Still at the door.*) Make it a dozen. Hurry!

SCHREIMANN: (*To ADLER.*) How bad is it?

PFLUGFELDER: (*Likewise.*) Why didn't you bring one with you?

Enter DR WENGER (previously PROFESSOR TUGENDVETTER's assistant, now Professor of Dermatology and Syphilis; thirty-ish; short; spectacles; troubled, insecure, sometimes a bit too loud). He has a newspaper in his pocket.

WENGER: Good evening, gentlemen.

SCHREIMANN: Look, he's got one! (*He pulls the paper out of WENGER's pocket.*) Thanks, Wenger.

WENGER: But – !

EBENWALD: Oh, how kind.

WENGER: Oh! I see! Is it the thing that the head of Dermatology and Syphilis brings the evening paper to the meetings? Professor Tugendvetter never said...

EBENWALD: (*At the paper.*) Here...here!

Everyone apart from ADLER and WENGER scrambles to look at the paper.

ADLER: What d'you think about all this, then?

WENGER: What can I think? I know nothing about politics. And I wasn't there on the day.

SCHREIMANN: Damn it, Ebenwald, read it out loud!

EBENWALD: Gentlemen. The wording of the question in the Lower House. 'We the undersigned Members consider it our duty – ' (*He stops.*)

PFLUGFELDER: Cat's got his tongue. Look, it's floored him. Give it to Professor Filitz – he's much more melodious than you are anyway.

EBENWALD: I always thought I was reasonably mel –

FILITZ: (*Grabbing the paper.*) ' – our duty to inform the Government of an incident' – et cetera – 'Father Franz Reder, priest at the Church of St Florian, was called to the deathbed of the critically ill Philomena Beier by a secular nurse, Ludmilla, in order to administer the last rites. In the ante-room to the ward, Father found a group of doctors, including Professor Bernhardi, head of' – et cetera – 'who, on the grounds that the dying woman might sustain damage to her health as a result of the excitement, curtly ordered the priest to desist – '

PFLUGFELDER: No, never – !

OTHERS: Shut up!

FILITZ: 'Professor Bernhardi (who is of the Mosaic denomination) was notified by His Reverend that he had come to fulfil a sacred duty, in this case imperative as (due to her own misdemeanours) the unmarried patient was suffering the consequences of an illegal interference, whereupon Professor jeeringly stressed his rights as master of the house – a house built and supported by noble philanthropists. When Father, refusing discussion, wanted to enter the ward, Professor blocked his path, and when Father touched the door handle, Professor gave him a shove…'

ADLER: That is a lie.

PFLUGFELDER: Filthy lie.

SCHREIMANN: You were there, were you?

FILITZ: As if a shove were the point.

EBENWALD: There are witnesses.

PFLUGFELDER: I know your sort of witness.

ADLER: I was there.

PFLUGFELDER: Then where's *your* account of what happened? How much of this is down to you, Ebenwald?

SCHREIMANN: Keep reading!

FILITZ: 'During this, patient died without receiving the consolations of religion, which, according to the nurse, she asked for. By notifying the Government, we ask the Minister for Education and Cultural Affairs how he intends to give satisfaction to the deeply injured Christian population of Vienna, and moreover if he doesn't think it fit, when it comes to the filling of public posts, to finally rule out men who, due to their education, character and descent, are incapable of showing understanding to the religious feelings of the indigenous Christian population.'

Commotion.

EBENWALD: Now the fat's really in the fire.

WENGER: Why? – there's not a word against us.

SCHREIMANN: Well said!

EBENWALD: Bravo, Wenger!

WENGER: (*Encouraged.*) No stain on the Institute's name.

PFLUGFELDER: And its Director?

WENGER: If he manages – and he will – to refute the aspersions –

PFLUGFELDER: *Aspersions*?! Dr Wenger, do you honestly need me to spell it out? This is a political straight thrust from *one* sabre held by a *coalition*: the clerics and the anti-Semites.

FILITZ: Horseshit!

EBENWALD: Here we go, the superannuated revolutionary is off on one. 'I remember back in 1848 – '

WENGER: Personally I don't recognise religious and national differences. I'm a scientist. I detest –

SCHREIMANN: Don't we all!

BERNHARDI and CYPRIAN enter. BERNHARDI has twelve copies of the newspaper. He is very cheerful. His manner is even more jocular and ironic than usual – though it's not entirely unselfconscious.

BERNHARDI: Evening, gentlemen! Who's sending nurses out to buy papers? D'you really need twelve? Sorry I'm late – hope you haven't been twiddling your thumbs.

General greetings. BERNHARDI sits at the head of the table. The rest sit. Some smoke.

I declare the meeting open. Before we start, let me extend a welcome to our new department head, Dr Wenger. You join us at an extraordinary time, doctor.

WENGER: Director. Colleagues. It'd be in poor taste to take up your precious time with a long speech –

FILITZ: Or a short one.

WENGER: So I'll simply thank each and every –

SCHREIMANN: (*Standing.*) Given the hour, I move that our colleague postpone his gratitude till a meeting at which I'm absent.

OTHERS: Hear hear!

SCHREIMANN shakes WENGER's hand, as do a few of the others.

BERNHARDI: Gentlemen, a full house, thank you.

ADLER: Löwenstein's missing.

BERNHARDI: Hopefully he'll be here soon. Your presence is proof of your devotion to the Institute. Occasionally, we have our differences, but that can't be helped in a large organisation – especially one like this, which has so many…well-known public figures.

Some disquiet.

Still, on the important issues, we're united – even if it raises the hackles of our enemies! Gentlemen, a letter from the Secretary of the Board, Privy Counsellor Winkler, hand-delivered to me this morning.

FILITZ: (*Mumbling.*) Finally.

BERNHARDI: 'Dear…' et cetera, 'I have the honour to inform you that the members of the Board have made the unanimous decision to relinquish their honorary positions…' and so on.

EBENWALD leans over the letter. BERNHARDI hands it to him. The letter circulates. BERNHARDI is smiling.

Take a look, everyone, nothing to hide. *Ipso facto* today's agenda is, what's our response? Professor Ebenwald desires the floor.

EBENWALD: I'd like to ask the Director if he knows *why* the Board has resigned? The letter's so curiously closed-mouthed.

PFLUGFELDER: (*Disgusted.*) Pah!

BERNHARDI: My answer's a question: who *doesn't* know? Since we all have plenty to be getting on with elsewhere –

CYPRIAN: Precisely!

BERNHARDI: – I'll fill the ignorant in by – oh, how convenient, by handing out a dozen copies of the paper. Oh, look, a *baker's* dozen! Page three: the question in Parliament.

SCHREIMANN: That has no place here.

BERNHARDI: It has no place in Parliament, even.

PFLUGFELDER: Well put!

BERNHARDI: It's because of something I did, and there are witnesses, and some of them are at this table, and they know today's bogus question is designed to serve the ends of a particular party –

FILITZ: Which one?

PFLUGFELDER: The anti-Semitic, clerical one!

FILITZ: Horseshit!

BERNHARDI: – a party whose character is known to all of us, whatever our private feelings about it might be –

PFLUGFELDER: Very good.

BERNHARDI: I'm not here to justify myself to anyone, I'm here as Director. Now how do we respond to the Board? Professor Cyprian has the floor.

CYPRIAN: (*Beginning monotonously.*) Several years ago on a pleasure trip of the Low Countries –

SCHREIMANN: (*Standing.*) Given the hour I respectfully ask that Cyprian postpone his anecdotes about dykes and get to the point.

CYPRIAN: Actually, it was an anecdote about a windmill, but have it your way. The Board's resigned. The reason – or pretext – we know. We also know that Bernhardi acted as a doctor on that day. Every one of us would have done the same thing.

FILITZ: Don't speak for me.

EBENWALD: You've never done it.

SCHREIMANN: And nor had Bernhardi – as far as we know.

CYPRIAN: Because such circumstances rarely arise. No one can deny that countless believers at death's door have found peace in the last rites – even non-believers. But the presence of a priest against the wishes of a dying person *or* the concerns of the doctor charged with his care, is an unacceptable ecclesiastical trespass. We've a duty to stop that, in certain cases. If you were acting on your conscience, you would have done what Bernhardi did. Yes, Ebenwald, you, and *you*, Filitz –

FILITZ: No!

CYPRIAN: Fear of the consequences might have moved you to let the priest in, nothing else. Bernhardi's mistake, if we can call it that, was that he held no such fear, that he followed his instinct as a doctor – we must applaud that. There's only one response to the Board: to unanimously pass a vote of confidence in our Director.

PFLUGFELDER: Bravo!

ADLER nods, though he looks undecided. WENGER looks to ADLER, then to the others.

BERNHARDI: The Vice-Director has the floor.

EBENWALD: I won't be hoodwinked: this is a monumental disaster. The fact is our patrons have abandoned us. And Professor Bernhardi is solely responsible.

BERNHARDI: I am.

EBENWALD: The ingratitude, lack of respect – for Board and Institute – if we declare our solidarity with him.

Some restlessness.

Yes, his behaviour wasn't malicious, but it *was* rash – and now we're facing ruin. I disagree with Cyprian. No vote of confidence in Bernhardi. Instead, I propose we express our regret at the incident and our condemnation of his behaviour.

The restlessness grows. He shouts.

I also propose that a plea be submitted to the Board to withdraw its resignation.

Great disquiet.

BERNHARDI: Gentlemen!

Unrest.

Please! Declarations of no confidence mean nothing to me – especially where I was able to predict them – and happily, I can also do without declarations of *confidence*. To stop you burning your bridges, I have to tell you we probably won't even need a Board shortly. I had a long conversation with His Excellency last night. In the short term, we can be confident of an ample subsidy;

in the long term, our nationalisation is under serious consideration.

EBENWALD: Shop-talk at the annual ball!

CYPRIAN: (*Rising.*) Now hang on – a few days ago I *also* spoke to His Excellency and –

FILITZ: Beside the point.

SCHREIMANN: Wishful thinking!

EBENWALD: A handout, in the middle of this mess!

FILITZ: After a parliamentary question? – damn fantasy!

Great unrest.

BERNHARDI: (*Forcefully.*) You seem to forget, gentlemen, that the question will get an *answer* from the Minister! Do you doubt him? He has the facts.

FILITZ: *All* of them?

SCHREIMANN: The Parliamentary question isn't the issue here!

FILITZ: Exactly. A motion's been proposed.

SCHREIMANN: So let's vote!

CYPRIAN: (*To BERNHARDI, quietly.*) Yes. Let's.

BERNHARDI: Two motions! One from Professor Ebenwald, namely –

LÖWENSTEIN enters.

LÖWENSTEIN: Gentlemen – I've come from Parliament!

Commotion.

Flint has answered the question!

EBENWALD: The vote, Bernhardi.

SCHREIMANN: (*Acting on LÖWENSTEIN's dismayed facial expression.*) Given the hour, I request an interruption.

BERNHARDI: (*Lightly.*) Everyone agreed? Excellent. Floor's yours, Löwenstein.

LÖWENSTEIN: A charge of religious agitation has been brought against you.

Commotion. All at once:

PFLUGFELDER: What!

CYPRIAN: Dr Löwenstein –

SCHREIMANN: Huh –!

ADLER: Religious agitation?

CYPRIAN: Speak up, man!

EBENWALD: Quiet! Please, Dr Löwenstein, can you be more explicit?

BERNHARDI is motionless.

LÖWENSTEIN: There's to be a criminal inquiry. It's enough to turn your stomach. You got what you wanted.

FILITZ: Let's not get personal.

CYPRIAN: Go on!

LÖWENSTEIN: It'll all be in tomorrow's papers.

SCHREIMANN: Löwenstein – try. A bit of context?

LÖWENSTEIN: Well…at first it looked as if the questioners were going to get it in the neck. His Excellency was very eloquent about Bernhardi's accomplishments…said he had no ulterior motives, that he was apolitical, that Austria was a meritocracy. And then the objections started – 'If only that were true!' 'The Jewification of the University!' – and suddenly the Minister began to, well, digress. He got very hot under the collar and soon he was on about the need for religious education and the marriage of Christianity and science. I'm convinced he was flabbergasted by his own right turn, but there it was: (*Mockingly.*) 'for the sake of House and country', 'meeting with Minister of Justice', 'inquiries against the Professor into the offence of religious agitation'.

PFLUGFELDER: What a disgrace.

FILITZ: How so?

CYPRIAN: And the response?

LÖWENSTEIN: Applause. Backslapping.

ADLER: Are you sure about this, Löwenstein?

LÖWENSTEIN: Feel free to disbelieve me.

CYPRIAN: Strictly speaking, it doesn't concern us at all.

FILITZ: Oh?

EBENWALD: We should continue the meeting.

BERNHARDI: (*Composed.*) I know I speak for everyone when I say, thank you, Dr Löwenstein, for the report. Order, please. As noted, the Parliamentary question, and its answer, are not for discussion. There are two motions.

EBENWALD: I withdraw mine.

Commotion. ADLER whispers an explanation to LÖWENSTEIN.

The Minister's answer has altered the lay of the land, so I assent to my motion's assimilation into a *new* motion.

CYPRIAN: The Minister's answer has nothing to do with anything in this room!

EBENWALD: I move for the suspension of Professor Bernhardi as Director of the Institute until the completion of the criminal inquiry against him.

Great commotion.

PFLUGFELDER: Shame on you, Ebenwald.

CYPRIAN: You don't even know if he's going to be charged yet.

LÖWENSTEIN: How offensive, how despicable!

CYPRIAN: You may have withdrawn your motion, mine stands. A vote of confidence in –

PFLUGFELDER: (*Interrupting.*) The bloody question in the house, its fucking answer – to hell with it, it's nothing to do with us!

EBENWALD: (*Roaring.*) Do we want to look like a herd of asses? Why settle anything tonight, when it'll probably be overturned by the law tomorrow!

CYPRIAN: Sorry, Ebenwald, but to quote Filitz: horseshit.

ADLER: Who has the right, dear prof, to void our resolutions?

LÖWENSTEIN: Bernhardi is and remains Director of this Institute. No one can remove him.

FILITZ: He's no longer Director in my eyes.

CYPRIAN: (*To BERNHARDI.*) My motion – a vote of confidence. Now.

Commotion.

BERNHARDI: Yes…according to order –

Disquiet.

ADLER: (*Very agitated.*) Everyone! They'll need my

testimony – I was there. Every witness knows the event was *not* depicted truthfully in the House. I'm deeply convinced of Bernhardi's innocence, I can testify to it –

BERNHARDI: Thank you.

ADLER: – and it's because of this I *welcome* an inquiry – all of us, irrespective of partisanship, *should* –

SCHREIMANN: There are no partisans in this hospital!

ADLER: This *has* to be clarified in public! We mustn't act pre-emptively, therefore I agree with the Vice-Director's motion that the Director be suspended –

Commotion.

FILITZ: Bit of common sense, at last!

ADLER: – and I ask everyone, especially Bernhardi, to see this as proof of my conviction that the inquiry will clear him completely.

CYPRIAN: But, Dr Adler, you're conceding that it's justified in the first place.

FILITZ: Who doesn't?

PFLUGFELDER: Flint's arse-licking the clericals! Stooge!

LÖWENSTEIN: Nothing new there.

CYPRIAN: (*To BERNHARDI.*) My motion!

BERNHARDI: Gentlemen!

Unrest.

SCHREIMANN: What – it's still a meeting? I was about to nip out for a game of billiards.

FILITZ: We should vote on Ebenwald's first.

BERNHARDI: I have a question for Professor Ebenwald.

FILITZ: Not allowed, according to the rules of procedure.

PFLUGFELDER: Oh, grow up.

EBENWALD: Please, go ahead.

BERNHARDI: You've proposed a motion for my suspension as a result of the Minister's answer. Did you know that I could have prevented the question?

LÖWENSTEIN: How *interesting.*

SCHREIMANN: Don't respond to that!

BERNHARDI: If you're half a man, Ebenwald, you will.

Commotion.

EBENWALD: Gentlemen. The professor's question is no surprise. Given how leading it was, pardon me if I don't answer him directly, but tell you why he asked it in the first place.

Unrest, anticipation.

Shortly after the *amusing* thing with the priest, I called on the Director to warn him that Parliament may use it against us. Some of you have no idea how to wrestle popular trends. It doesn't matter whether they're defensible, philosophically, institutions like ours *have* to wrestle them. Put simply, given that we have an archduke and a bishop on our Board, and that statistically eighty-five per cent of our patients are Catholic, there are people who think it wrong that the majority of our doctors belong to a different denomination. It breeds bad blood.

LÖWENSTEIN: Funny how eighty per cent of the cash we get comes from this 'other' denomination.

EBENWALD: Not the point. The patients are the point. As you know, recently there was dialogue about Professor

Tugendvetter's replacement: should it be Dr Hell or Dr Wenger (hello, there). Now, picture it, gentlemen, a good friend comes to you –

PFLUGFELDER: Or a cousin –

EBENWALD: – could be cousin – comes and says, 'Hmn, might look a bit fishy, electing another Jew, with this embarrassing incident the talk of Vienna. Parliament might pounce'. Was it so wrong of me to go to the Director and say, 'Let's appoint Dr Hell,' – who's no slouch, after all – 'in order to side-step more mess'?

WENGER: Quite right!

Laughter.

EBENWALD: Well, there you have it. I *could* have asked Wenger to withdraw, but I'm no conspirator, so I went to the top. That's why Bernhardi asked his not-so-flummoxing question. And it's true, we might not be talking about questions in the House tonight if Dr Hell were sitting there. Instead it's Wenger and we're knee-deep in it.

PFLUGFELDER: Bravo, Bernhardi!

BERNHARDI: Gentlemen, Professor Ebenwald has answered in the style of a popular ditty; lots of tuneful folksiness, truth utterly lost. I'm not going to defend myself for not doing business with a deal-maker –

SCHREIMANN: Now hang –

BERNHARDI: If you call me a 'religious agitator', I call Ebenwald a 'deal-maker'.

PFLUGFELDER: Precisely.

BERNHARDI: But it doesn't matter: *mea culpa*, I confess, guilty! Guilty that as Director I didn't do everything I could to stop a manœuvre in Parliament designed to belittle us in the eyes of frauds and fools. I accept the consequences, and I hereby tender my resignation.

Chaos.

CYPRIAN: What are you doing?

LÖWENSTEIN: No, stop – you mustn't!

PFLUGFELDER: That requires a vote!

BERNHARDI: What for? In favour of my suspension: Professors Ebenwald, Filitz, Drs Schreimann, Adler –

LÖWENSTEIN: Only four!

BERNHARDI: I'm sparing Dr Wenger the moral dilemma. He might vote for me because I voted for him – and I don't want to have to lay the rather dubious honour of being your Director at his feet.

SCHREIMANN: What a nasty remark.

FILITZ: Out of line, Bernhardi.

PFLUGFELDER: You're to blame for this, Adler.

LÖWENSTEIN: It must be voted on.

PFLUGFELDER: It's desertion!

BERNHARDI: Desertion?

CYPRIAN: You can't leave before a vote.

BERNHARDI: I won't allow it, I won't be judged.

FILITZ: Too late for that.

SCHREIMANN: Have you resigned or haven't you?

BERNHARDI: I have.

SCHREIMANN: Then Professor Ebenwald is Acting Director and chairman of this meeting.

LÖWENSTEIN: This is going too far.

FILITZ: (*To Schreimann.*) You're right.

PFLUGFELDER: We don't have to stomach this –

CYPRIAN: Bernhardi...Bernhardi!

EBENWALD: Professor Bernhardi has, alas, resigned, so in line with our statute (paragraph seven, clause three), I am your Acting Director. I hope I have your loyalty: I hope I shall prove worthy: I give Professor Filitz the floor.

LÖWENSTEIN: This is sickening.

PFLUGFELDER: You are *not* Director, Professor Ebenwald, not yet!

Unrest.

FILITZ: Question now is who's going to take over Bernhardi's department?

CYPRIAN: What are you talking about?

PFLUGFELDER: You're very *limited*, really, aren't you, Filitz?

BERNHARDI: I'm still a member of the Institute, gentlemen, and head of my department.

ADLER: Goes without saying.

WENGER: Yes, absolutely.

SCHREIMANN: I think it could get a bit sticky, actually, were the suspended Director to –

LÖWENSTEIN: He's not suspended.

CYPRIAN: He tendered his resignation.

FILITZ: Not exactly voluntarily.

PFLUGFELDER: He chucked it square at *your* repellent chump, Filitz!

EBENWALD: Shut up, gentlemen!

BERNHARDI: (*Having completely lost his self-control.*) Nobody has the right to force me from my department! But I'll take leave till this is settled.

CYPRIAN: What are you doing?

EBENWALD: Leave approved.

BERNHARDI: Thank you! While I'm away, I entrust my department to my assistants, Dr Kurt Pflugfelder and Dr Oskar Bernhardi.

EBENWALD: No objection here.

BERNHARDI: Good night, gentlemen.

LÖWENSTEIN: Ditto.

CYPRIAN takes his hat.

BERNHARDI: Oh, no – they'd *love* that. Please stay.

PFLUGFELDER: *You* stay, Bernhardi.

BERNHARDI: Here?

ADLER: Slightly concerned, prof, you've got the wrong end of the stick. I'd like to say for the record how much I admire you.

BERNHARDI: Thank you very much. You're either with me, or you're against me. Good night.

He exits. There is mounting disquiet.

PFLUGFELDER: (*Often having to shout.*) You're going to let him walk? For the last time: have you lost your minds? Don't do it! Forget the feud: think back to how this whole damn thing started. The girl thought she was cured – the sweetest moment of her life. And Bernhardi didn't want to disabuse her. *That's* what he's guilty of! He asked the priest to let that poor child die peacefully. *Asked.* You all know it. Whose religious feelings were truly offended? And if they were, how much of it's down to the scandal-mongers in all of their warped, career-hungry ugliness? It's in their *interest* that religious feelings *should* be offended. Would it have been possible to concoct anything from this, without politics? We're *doctors* – why play along with this ludicrous pantomime, with its pro and con, left and right, lies, hoaxes, boot-licking? He acted on his gut; I'm not saying it's heroic, just human. Be men. Forget tonight. Ask Bernhardi to accept his position back – there's no man more worthy. Make him return, gentlemen, I urge you, make him return!

EBENWALD: End of aria, Professor Pflugfelder? *Coloratura cadenza* to finish? Apparently not. The agenda, gentlemen.

PFLUGFELDER: Good night.

CYPRIAN: *Adieu.*

LÖWENSTEIN: You're no longer a quorum.

SCHREIMANN: We're not jumping ship.

FILITZ: If it's left to us to make decisions without you, so be it.

PFLUGFELDER: (*Opening the door.*) Mr Hochroitzpointner, in the nick of time!

LÖWENSTEIN: Night-night, Mr Vice-Director. I'll send for beer and sluts.

PFLUGFELDER: Enjoy it. You deserve each other.

CYPRIAN, PFLUGFELDER and LÖWENSTEIN exit.

EBENWALD: Did you want something, Mr
  Hochroitzpointner?

HOCHROITZPOINTNER: (*Standing in the door.*) Um –

EBENWALD: Go on then, close the door!

HOCHROITZPOINTNER closes it.

Now. Where were we?

End of Act Three.

Act Four

The reception-room at BERNHARDI's home. Two doors: one to the hall and one to the dining-room. PFLUGFELDER has just entered.

LÖWENSTEIN: (*Off.*) Professor Pflugfelder!

He enters.

PFLUGFELDER: Lost your breath, Löwenstein!?

LÖWENSTEIN: I've been chasing you for half a mile. Well?

PFLUGFELDER: Weren't you in court?

LÖWENSTEIN: I kept being called out. So?

PFLUGFELDER: Two months.

LÖWENSTEIN: What – ! But the priest, his testimony!

PFLUGFELDER: Helped the priest, not Bernhardi.

LÖWENSTEIN: But –

PFLUGFELDER: Yes I know, Father didn't feel he was *shoved*, more *tapped* on the shoulder... The prosecution twisted it: 'very charitable of you to describe it thus, father; a case in point of Christian clemency, gentlemen'. The whole priesthood got a pat on the back for that tap.

LÖWENSTEIN: So it was Hochroitzpointner who put him away – and that panic-stricken nurse, Ludmilla. All the other witness evidence cleared him! I'll have to say sorry to Adler – I didn't expect that! And Cyprian! And Kurt!

CYPRIAN enters. Greetings.

PFLUGFELDER: Where is he?

LÖWENSTEIN: They didn't take him off straight away, did they?

CYPRIAN: No, he's with his lawyer.

PFLUGFELDER: Mmn, we could have done without him.

LÖWENSTEIN: You don't say.

CYPRIAN: Without a defence?

PFLUGFELDER: Without *Goldenthal*'s defence.

CYPRIAN: What have you got against him? He spoke extremely well. Not very aggressive, but –

PFLUGFELDER: Forelock-tugging flunkey!

LÖWENSTEIN: Toad. No surprise.

CYPRIAN: Oh?

LÖWENSTEIN: Christened! Convert! The wife wears a cross, son goes to Catholic school.

CYPRIAN: Ah, your infamous *idée fixe*!

LÖWENSTEIN: With a different defence we'd have had a different outcome.

CYPRIAN: With a different accused we might have. If anyone didn't help Bernhardi in there, it was Bernhardi. I don't want to be too critical of him, but even his most loyal supporters couldn't say he was particularly clever.

LÖWENSTEIN: What are you talking about? – if you ask me, he was breathtaking. He even kept a cool head during that bastard Hochroitzpointner's lies.

CYPRIAN: He wasn't cool-headed, he was defiant.

PFLUGFELDER: (*To CYPRIAN.*) He missed half of it. (*To LÖWENSTEIN.*) Bernhardi tried to summon Professor Ebenwald.

LÖWENSTEIN: Ah.

CYPRIAN: And Minister Flint.

LÖWENSTEIN: Genius!

CYPRIAN: Don't be ridiculous – Flint and Ebenwald have nothing to do with it. He might as well have summoned his nanny.

KURT enters.

PFLUGFELDER: Kurt! (*He embraces him.*)

KURT: Hello, Father.

LÖWENSTEIN: (*To CYPRIAN.*) How touching it is.

CYPRIAN: Take your hat off: this young man publicly branded Mr Hochroitzpointner a liar!

LÖWENSTEIN: What?

CYPRIAN: And was fined two hundred crowns for it.

LÖWENSTEIN: Oh, Dr Pflugfelder, allow *me* a kiss!

KURT: Cheers, Dr Löwenstein, consider me kissed.

LÖWENSTEIN: At least let me contribute to the fine, you magnificent man!

PFLUGFELDER: They'll get their money. Kurt, if you're thinking of duelling Hochroitzpointner –

KURT: Where's the nearest council of honour, I'm up for it.

LÖWENSTEIN: He won't dare.

KURT: Mmn, he'll crawl off under a rock before I get the chance, I suppose. Well I haven't finished with him, even if they've finished with Bernhardi.

CYPRIAN: Let's hope it's not over yet.

Enter DR GOLDENTHAL (forty-five; corpulent, curly hair, greying, black side-burns; dignified, a little unctuous and nasal.).

GOLDENTHAL: Good evening, gentlemen.

LÖWENSTEIN: Dr Goldenthal – where's your client?

GOLDENTHAL: I recommended he leave court through a back door.

LÖWENSTEIN: Cheering crowds outside the front, hmn?

GOLDENTHAL: Patience, gentlemen: that might yet happen. We didn't win today, but it was an honourable loss.

PFLUGFELDER: For those of us not being flung in gaol, absolutely.

GOLDENTHAL: (*Laughing.*) A little jibe at me, professor? Well…it mightn't yet come to that… In all seriousness, as we have a moment – I'd like to ask for your support. The man's a bit, well, stubborn. Summoning the minister…that obstinate silence…none of it went down well. And now he wants to keep playing the injured party. Of course I want to appeal. He won't hear of it!

CYPRIAN: I thought this might happen.

LÖWENSTEIN: What would be the point?

PFLUGFELDER: What we need is to get this out in the world, to petition the public.

GOLDENTHAL: Pardon, professor, but the trial didn't take place behind closed doors.

PFLUGFELDER: I mean get to *real* Austrians. The crazy thing is we've kept our traps shut all this time. Look at our opponent party! Did the clerical papers wait till the verdict before they splashed their opinions across their front pages? Course not, they slandered him in every edition because they were the ones who took this so-called offence and distorted it into a 'crime' in the first place. And the liberal papers played by the rules.

LÖWENSTEIN: They're civilised, aren't they?

PFLUGFELDER: I can think of other descriptions. Why worry about the colour of your foes, when your friends are yellow?

CYPRIAN: You want to talk to 'real' Austrians? The jury, Pflugfelder. Not real enough for you?

PFLUGFELDER: Oh, very; they just didn't hear the truth in plain-spoken language.

GOLDENTHAL: Well!

PFLUGFELDER: Call me a bloody fool, but I believe in the basic sense of right and wrong in ordinary people – people who've never been near a courthouse.

LÖWENSTEIN: We should call public meetings!

CYPRIAN: Watch: open discussion of Bernhardi will be banned.

PFLUGFELDER: Federal elections are round the corner.

CYPRIAN: What, are you standing?

PFLUGFELDER: No, but I'll demonstrate.

CYPRIAN: What with? Hackneyed speeches?

PFLUGFELDER: If I have to. Our enemies deny the simple truth. What else can we do except shout it from every rooftop? If that makes us phrasemongers, then phrasemongers we are; damn the bloody snobs to hell; we can't give in to lies and liars.

LÖWENSTEIN: Actually, we should seriously consider

if, in the interests of the cause, it'd be a *good* thing for Bernhardi to do his two months.

Laughter.

PFLUGFELDER: It'd highlight the disgrace of what they've done to him.

BERNHARDI and OSKAR enter. BERNHARDI is in a good mood, having heard the laughter.

BERNHARDI: Good, a party, count me in – sorry not to have been here earlier.

Handshakes.

CYPRIAN: So you escaped the cheering crowds?

BERNHARDI: Not exactly. A few, um, gentlemen, were ready and waiting with a dramatic reception, even at the back door.

LÖWENSTEIN: How dramatic?

BERNHARDI: 'Down with the Jews!' 'Down with the Freemasons!'

LÖWENSTEIN: About time – down with the Freemasons!

The doorbell rings. OSKAR makes to leave; BERNHARDI detains him.

BERNHARDI: You'll stay to dinner, gentlemen? See if there's enough, Oskar. My housekeeper walked out on me. Her confessor said under no circumstances could she stay – too dangerous to the good of her soul. A small spread, as befits a gaolbird. Oh, Oskar, no tears. (*Gently.*) Don't be sentimental.

OSKAR: I'm angry, that's all.

He exits and returns shortly after. ADLER enters.

ADLER: Door was open.

BERNHARDI: Greetings, Dr Adler! Give me one repentant sinner over ninety-nine righteous men!

ADLER: (*Agreeably.*) Not a sinner, professor. As I said, we had to have this trial. Though I'd no idea Cyprian and I would be seen as less reliable witnesses than Mr Hoch, Hoch, Hochroitzpointner.

CYPRIAN: The priest himself didn't fare much better –

GOLDENTHAL: The priest, gentlemen! An historic moment! To say – in response to my question, of course – to say our friend hadn't intended hostility towards the Catholic church, and for it not to help us one iota! If anything proved a certain movement is extremely powerful, that did.

BERNHARDI: If he was scared of said movement, his testimony would have been different.

GOLDENTHAL: You're not suggesting a servant of the church would deliberately lie?

PFLUGFELDER: Shock, horror.

ADLER: You know, Bernhardi, you're being unfair. I think he likes you. He's no ordinary man. Even back on the ward, I felt that.

BERNHARDI: Like? When 'like' is attached to risk, I believe in it.

GOLDENTHAL: What favours has he done himself or his career? We'll need that man again. When justice has been done to you, perhaps you'll judge him justly.

BERNHARDI: I've already told you, I won't stand in front of these people again. It'd be a waste of time, and you know it.

GOLDENTHAL: Not at all: it's impossible to predict what might happen in a higher court...

PFLUGFELDER: The higher you go, the worse their behaviour.

GOLDENTHAL: ...and you must have noticed certain changes in the political climate recently...

LÖWENSTEIN: Yes, things are getting worse.

GOLDENTHAL: No, a liberal wind is blowing in our fatherland, I can feel it. By the time we have a new trial –

BERNHARDI: But what could I get, Dr Goldenthal? An acquittal? Justice? Even with that, I'd still be a long way from square with the likes of Flint and Ebenwald.

GOLDENTHAL: I've already told you, there's no judicial proof those men have wronged you.

BERNHARDI: I don't need judicial proof.

GOLDENTHAL: But we couldn't build a case against them in a legal sense.

BERNHARDI: Which is exactly why I'm refusing to pursue it in court.

GOLDENTHAL: Please...it's my duty to warn you not to do anything stupid. (*Generally.*) All of you, take note. (*To BERNHARDI.*) Your blood's boiling...understandable... But you don't want to be charged with something else.

BERNHARDI: I know where the truth lies.

PFLUGFELDER: Whatever you're planning, count me in.

LÖWENSTEIN: And me. I say the whole system needs a hit.

GOLDENTHAL: Gentlemen, you can't –

LÖWENSTEIN: You trusted Flint.

PFLUGFELDER: Crony to the clerics, ought to be hounded to hell!

LÖWENSTEIN: And have you heard what's coming?
– compulsory confession for schoolchildren. A new
Catholic university. Scientist? – pah! Minister for
Education and Hypocrisy! The whole system will be
swamped with presumptuous padres!

GOLDENTHAL: At the risk of annoying you even further,
I don't have any objections to those measures.

LÖWENSTEIN: Well, the new Catholic university will
be a hop, skip and jump from your son's new Catholic
school, won't it!

GOLDENTHAL: The best school in Austria, doctor.
You malign the clerics. Many do. But I always say that
amongst them are men of real intellectual and spiritual
standing; some of them were in court today. My motto
has always been, respect the convictions of your enemy,
even in the midst of the most hostile battle.

LÖWENSTEIN: Minister Flint?! Convictions?

GOLDENTHAL: He has a duty to protect *all* convictions.
There are some things you shouldn't touch, gentlemen.

PFLUGFELDER: People with the courage to touch the
'untouchable' are people who move the world.

GOLDENTHAL: Moving the world wasn't Bernhardi's
objective – ask him yourself.

LÖWENSTEIN: Perhaps one day we'll see that's just what
he did do.

BERNHARDI: Oh, no – ! What are you saying – ?

GOLDENTHAL: Anyway, it's not my job to make politics
but to defend.

PFLUGFELDER: If only you'd done that.

BERNHARDI: Pflugfelder –!

GOLDENTHAL: Please, professor, now it's getting interesting. You don't think I defended my client?

PFLUGFELDER: Dr Goldenthal, if Austria needed to believe that the entire Catholic world, from the Pope to the village bigot, was offended by Bernhardi, all she had to do was pin her ears back to your defence! The judges entered with the conviction typed up in their briefcases; you spared them the nuisance of having to change the paperwork by calling it an act of rashness – which is *not* what it was, it was the act of a *doctor*. Yes, the jurors were venomous asses, but you treated them as the brains in Austria's top drawer, so they never wavered; and you coddled Hochroitzpointner and that nurse. Anyone would think that you *believed* in the imperative of the sacrament Bernhardi is supposed to have offended – at one point you even hinted that Bernhardi's got it wrong by not believing it himself! You practically prostrated yourself in front of his enemies. If my friend is happy with this, that's his business, but it's not defence in my book.

GOLDENTHAL: Stick to medicine, doctor. With your temper and knowledge of the law, you'd bring the most innocent man to prison.

LÖWENSTEIN: A feat *you* managed, sir.

BERNHARDI: That's enough!

The doorbell rings. OSKAR exits.

GOLDENTHAL: Bernhardi, happy the fellow who can call friends like these his own. I wouldn't dream of forcing my advice on you a second longer, and leave it up to you –

CYPRIAN: (*To PFLUGFELDER.*) Now look what you've done.

BERNHARDI: (*To GOLDENTHAL.*) What are you talking about?

PFLUGFELDER: I'm the one who should go. I'm sorry, Bernhardi, got carried away. But I don't regret a word.

He exits. OSKAR enters, somewhat ashen-faced. He whispers to BERNHARDI. BERNHARDI is shaken. He hesitates. He wants to turn towards CYPRIAN, but changes his mind.

BERNHARDI: I'm sorry, gentlemen, a visitor… I can't turn him away. Hopefully he won't… Oskar, please… the dining-room… Make yourselves at…

CYPRIAN: What's the matter?

BERNHARDI: Later.

OSKAR shows KURT, LÖWENSTEIN, ADLER, CYPRIAN and GOLDENTHAL into the dining-room. BERNHARDI closes the door after them. OSKAR exits to the hall and returns with the PRIEST.

Please, come in –

PRIEST: Good evening, professor.

BERNHARDI: Thank you, Oskar.

OSKAR exits to the hall.

Here to give me your condolences, father?

PRIEST: No, not exactly. But I need to speak to you tonight.

BERNHARDI: Please. I'm all ears.

He offers him a chair, and they both sit.

PRIEST: Not a good day for you, professor…but…I think it's obvious I'm not to blame.

BERNHARDI: Father, I won't insult you by thanking you for telling the truth under oath.

PRIEST: (*Already somewhat put out.*) I'm not here for thanks…even though I *did* say more than I needed…

and I'm not going to regurgitate it...because I want to go even...I want to make another concession to you.

BERNHARDI looks at him enquiringly.

Today I said you weren't motivated by explicit hostility towards me or the Catholic church. Now I also have to allow that in this case – understand me, professor: in this particular case – you also acted correctly in your capacity as doctor. You had your responsibilities, as I had mine, and you couldn't have acted differently.

BERNHARDI: You think...I acted correctly? That I couldn't have acted differently?

PRIEST: You couldn't have acted differently as a doctor.

BERNHARDI: (*After a pause.*) I have to say, father, you had a better opportunity to get this off your chest a couple of hours ago.

PRIEST: Not through lack of nerve – or why would I be here?

BERNHARDI: Then –

PRIEST: Let me finish. In court, I had an insight, a revelation, really. One *more* word from me and I would have done damage...untold damage...to a holy cause... to me, the *most* holy.

BERNHARDI: What could be holier than the truth?

PRIEST: Professor. You can't mean there's nothing holier than the puny 'truth' in this one case? No, no. I admitted, publicly, your good intention – and many well-meaning people will never forgive me for going *that* far. If I'd *also* conceded it was your *right* to send me away from that woman, a Christian, a sinner, then the enemies of my church would have seized it and twisted it to their own ends. Compassion would have become treason; the slight 'truth' would have become a wider lie; I'd have been a traitor to my church and God. That's why I didn't say it in court.

BERNHARDI: So why say it now?

PRIEST: Because when I had the revelation, I promised myself I'd come here. The world wouldn't have understood – but I owe it to you.

BERNHARDI: Thank you, father. Here's hoping you never have to publicly testify in a case with more at stake than...than *me*! You could have your private doubts – I mean your divine revelation – and end up butchering an even higher truth than the one you think you have to protect.

PRIEST: But the highest truth is the truth of my church. And my church's first rule is obedience. Loyalty. It's different for men like you. The church throws a blanket of blessing over the world – if I were thrown out, my life would have no meaning.

BERNHARDI: Father, there have been many priests who found meaning *after* they left. They told the truth freely, no fear of backlash.

PRIEST: If I belonged to them, God would have made me say in court the things I've said here.

BERNHARDI: Oh, *God* buttoned your lips? And God's sent you round to mine for your confidential confession – though *publicly* it was taboo? Your God makes it very easy for you, doesn't he!

PRIEST: (*Rising.*) I'm sorry, professor, I don't have anything else to say. You seem bent on reading this as an admission of wrong-doing. I never intended it to lead to an argument.

BERNHARDI: And so you slam the door in my face? I don't accept that as proof of anything. I'm sorry you came here for nothing.

PRIEST: (*Not without irony.*) Nothing?

BERNHARDI: I can't forgive you as much as you might have expected.

PRIEST: I didn't come here for forgiveness. Perhaps solace. And I have that...yes. I'm beginning to see this whole thing in a new light. I was wrong about the real reason I came...was *sent.*

BERNHARDI: Oh?

PRIEST: It wasn't to concede anything! It was to free myself from a doubt. I hardly realised I even had it – and now it's vanished! I see what I was meant to see, at last! I withdraw my concession.

BERNHARDI: You withdraw it? But I've taken it.

PRIEST: It's invalid. You were wrong when you sent me away from that dying child's bed.

BERNHARDI: Ah!

PRIEST: *You* were wrong. I know that now. Others might have been right in the same position, but not you. Apparently you stopped me on the grounds of 'medical care', 'human compassion'. You didn't: they were pretexts. Perhaps not conscious ones, but pretexts, all the same.

BERNHARDI: Let me get this right: one minute you say I had my responsibilities – as you had yours. Now you've changed your mind?

PRIEST: You had your responsibilities, but now I don't accept you stopped me *purely* on the grounds you claim. Perhaps you think you did – I was close to believing it myself. But no. The real reason is deeper. Rooted at the base of your soul. You...you dislike me. You...hate me –

BERNHARDI: Hate –?

PRIEST: – hate this cloth and what it means to you…and men like you. You can't hide it. I felt the heat of it then, I feel it now. Everything, your posture, your words… hate. The hatred men like you have for men like me.

BERNHARDI: 'Hate', 'hate' – and if it were true? If I'm really capable of such a thing in the first place, mightn't it be justified after everything I've been through, the smear campaign, which *you* think shameful? I can't deny it, despite my infuriating propensity for justice, I *have* felt something like it – but not because of *you*, because of the circus around you. Father, I swear, when I barred you from that ward, there wasn't a breath of hate in me. I faced you as a doctor, my heart pure, as pure as any member of your profession's, as pure as yours. You knew that earlier, you admitted it. Now you're denying it…because you feel…you feel the same thing I feel, I've never felt it more intensely: something divides us. We couldn't deceive ourselves about it even in friendlier circumstances.

PRIEST: You feel it now more than ever?

BERNHARDI: Yes, this second, as I stand face-to-face with you – and *you're* a free-thinking churchman. It'll separate us forever, this thing…I'm sorry, but 'hate' doesn't tell us what it is. It's much bigger. Bigger…and more hopeless.

PRIEST: Perhaps you're right. Hopeless. I've walked into this dangerous territory before, with scholars… enlightened thinkers… (*Somewhat mockingly.*) but dialogue has never felt this impossible. Perhaps I shouldn't have followed you this far, today of all days.

BERNHARDI: Father, I hope you respect me enough not to put my world-view down to a bad mood at the prospect of two months in the clink?

PRIEST: That didn't even occur to me... An unbridgeable abyss. But if we're both free of (*Smiling.*) hate, its cause must be very deep. Now I see communication is possible between faith and doubt...but not – you won't misunderstand me, given everything you've said – not between humility and presumption.

BERNHARDI: Presumption? The thing at the root of my soul is 'presumption'? You can't think of a softer word – yet you don't hate men like me?

PRIEST: (*Wanting to become heated; tempering himself; smiling, almost imperceptibly.*) I don't, I know it. My religion tells me to love those who hate me.

BERNHARDI: (*Forcefully.*) And mine – or the thing that fastens itself to my heart in its place – to understand, even when I'm misunderstood.

PRIEST: You're well-intentioned, but understanding has limits. The mind deceives us, it plays tricks – you know that. But men like me can *never* be deceived by – (*He hesitates.*) I want to land on a phrase to which you won't object, professor – by our inner sense.

BERNHARDI: Let's both land on that. I try to trust this 'inner sense' as well, even though mine probably springs from a different part of my soul. What else *can* we do in the end? And if...it's harder for men like me than men like you...well, God, who created you so humble and me so...presumptuous...surely has His own mysterious reasons.

The PRIEST looks at him for a long time. With a sudden decision, he holds out his hand. BERNHARDI hesitates, and then, with an almost imperceptible smile:

Across the abyss, father?

PRIEST: We'd better not look down, not even for a second!

BERNHARDI shakes the PRIEST's hand.

Goodbye, professor!

He exits. BERNHARDI is alone. He reflects, and seems undecided. Then his knitted brow smoothes itself over, and he makes a movement as if he were shaking something off. OSKAR appears at the door.

OSKAR: Father?

BERNHARDI: Come in, Oskar.

OSKAR: There's a journalist from *The Chronicle* at the door.

BERNHARDI: I've already been executed.

OSKAR: And the Chairman of the Society of Free-thinkers of Brigittenau.

BERNHARDI: I'm in the dungeon.

OSKAR: And telegrams. (*He holds them out.*)

BERNHARDI: I'm a doctor, Oskar. I want to put this behind me. I haven't done what I'm on this earth to do for months. Meetings, interrogations, and for what? I heal, or try to; that's what I do, and that's what I want to return to as soon as possible. No appeal, send me to gaol, I want to start my punishment. Tomorrow, if the room's ready. (*He opens the door to the dining-room and makes his way in.*) Gentlemen...!

End of Act Four.

Act Five

A well-appointed office at the Ministry of Education and Cultural Affairs. PRIVY COUNSELLOR WINKLER (forty-five, fresh face, blue eyes, slim; short, blond and greying hair, neat moustache) is at his desk, finishing a phone-call.

WINKLER: ...no, he won't be in Parliament till half-past one. It'll be our pleasure, Professor Ebenwald. See you shortly.

He hangs up. A SECRETARY enters.

SECRETARY: A gentleman, privy counsellor, from *The Chronicle*. He wants to speak to His Excellency in person.

WINKLER: Tell him to come back later.

SECRETARY: Two other journalists keep calling, sir. One about yesterday's elections, the other –

WINKLER: There's no need to keep announcing the press to me. It's His Excellency they want to speak to, isn't it?

SECRETARY: Yes, privy counsellor.

The telephone rings. The SECRETARY answers.

The offices of the Imperial Ministry for Cultural Affairs and Education? Yes. One moment. Mr Bermann from the Ministry of Justice.

She hands him the phone and exits.

WINKLER: Bermann – how's life in the courts? (*Very surprised.*) What? Don't be ridiculous, Nurse Ludmilla? Why would she want a meeting? Really? I tell you, it's a coincidence. Because Professor Bernhardi's released from prison today. Yes! If you don't *want* me to tell His Excellency, I won't. Goodbye!

He hangs up. He seems agitated, momentarily. FLINT enters.

FLINT: Hello, Winkler.

WINKLER: Excellency. Professor Ebenwald just rang. He's on his way.

FLINT: Can't keep away from the place, can he?

WINKLER: The Elisabeth Institute is, well, penniless.

FLINT: But the Board came back on, er, board, didn't they, after Bernhardi's removal?

WINKLER: Yes, but it turns out the only one who could keep the Board awake was Bernhardi.

FLINT: Aren't you on the Board?

WINKLER: Oh, yes.

FLINT: A subsidy. I promised my friend that. You know, back then.

WINKLER: The figures are rather large, Excellency. We could milk the Minister of Finance for three grand, though he might get stroppy.

FLINT: I'll demand a separate loan in Parliament.

WINKLER: Oh?

FLINT: I'll get it. The Social Democrats and Liberals can't start getting stingy over the sustenance of scientific institutes, can they? As for the Christian Socials and clericals, I think I have the right to expect some tit for tat. They do owe me one, I believe.

WINKLER: Yes, Excellency. They certainly do.

FLINT: Stop being supercilious. The only thing that matters in public life, Winkler, is balanced books. (*Casually regarding the newspapers on WINKLER's desk.*) Any news?

WINKLER: (*Lightly.*) Ten new Social Democrat mandates at yesterday's Federal elections.

FLINT: Real turn-up, congratulations, you leftists must be over the moon. Anything else?

WINKLER: Um...well... Oh! Yes, congratulations on yesterday's speech, sir.

FLINT: That old thing? Did the job. Remarkably unbiased of you, Winkler, to join the chorus of approval. I didn't put you down as being in favour of a more robust programme of religious education.

WINKLER: Are *you* in favour, Excellency?

FLINT: What I think about these matters in private is a completely different chapter in the book, privy counsellor. Leave it to dilettantes to jabber out opinions. The melody of conviction's very thin-sounding. In politics, what counts is, er, counterpoint. (*More seriously.*) But don't assume it's easy. Take Bernhardi. It was a sacrifice to throw my old friend into the jaws of those sharks. But it was necessary – all there for the record. And if the day comes when I have to shake off certain hangers-on...well, it *will* become clear that I'm *not* the Minister for Cultural Affairs and Catholics, as some hack branded me today.

WINKLER: Mmn.

FLINT: Tickles your funny-bone, hmn? He's coining the phrase. Pflugfelder authored it at one of those uncalled-for meetings where the Bernhardi affair numbers one to sixty on the agenda. The government representatives are a bit lax at those things, aren't they?

WINKLER: *That* meeting was dissolved, Excellency, you can't ask for more.

FLINT: Only when Pflugfelder started dressing down the Archbishop for transferring the priest in question to a far-flung parish on the Polish border.

WINKLER: Correct.

FLINT: Damn the whole bloody thing! Bernhardi this, Bernhardi that – now even the liberal press has lost all restraint, they're practically martyring him as the victim of a popish plot, the Dreyfus of the Hospitals. Did you read the editorial in *The Chronicle*? Of course you did, it's your favourite rag! Positive glee at his release! The cheek!

WINKLER: I'm against all newspapers. And an editorial is hardly Professor Bernhardi's fault.

FLINT: Well, if he *does* give in to his friends' rabble-rousing, he'll come out smelling of shit. I'm not going to lie back and allow insurrection, and nor's the Minister of Justice, with whom I had a chit-chat yesterday. Faced with law-breaking, we'll apply the full force of the, er, law. I'd be sorry for Bernhardi, then. He hasn't behaved wisely and he's caused me a lot of – (*He taps his heart.*) – pain – but, still, he's not a bad sort. Always thought that, always will.

WINKLER: Friends of youth.

FLINT: Don't start gushing about youth, Winkler. Bernhardi and I were bright-eyed medical students together quarter of a century ago, but it adds up to sweet nothing. Damn the heart. Stride over corpses… Yes, you heard me.

The SECRETARY enters with a card.

WINKLER: Professor Ebenwald.

FLINT: Let him in.

The SECRETARY exits.

How much can we scrape together for the Institute, again?

WINKLER: Three grand.

EBENWALD enters. He bows.

FLINT: Morning, professor. How's the directorship?

EBENWALD: Acting only, Excellency. It's not out of the question that Professor Bernhardi will be re-elected in the coming days. It was only a suspension.

WINKLER: By law, he's stripped of his professorship and doctorhood.

EBENWALD: I'm sure they'll turn a blind eye. Thanks to his friends and parts of the press, there seems to have been a seismic shift in public opinion. One of my students just told me he's been escorted to his home in triumph.

FLINT: What the hell does 'in triumph' mean?

EBENWALD: Apparently a large group of students greeted him at the prison doors with cheers.

FLINT: All we need now's a pageant.

WINKLER: Would take some organising, Excellency – should I make some calls?

EBENWALD: Could I suggest that the demonstration and the general elation of the Social Democrats at their success in yesterday's elections are connected?

FLINT: Oh? Yes! You could suggest it! You see, Winkler? We shouldn't read anything consequential into this… triumphaliberalism. I'm sure they were all Zionists.

EBENWALD: They *do* have a certain amount of clout in Austria.

FLINT: Hmn. (*He changes the subject.*) You're here about the subsidy?

EBENWALD: Yes, Excellency.

FLINT: Sadly, we can only give you a gobbet of what you're expecting. To make up for it, I can tell you that the nationalisation of your Institute is under serious consideration.

EBENWALD: Excellency, I wonder when 'consideration' might become 'decision'?

FLINT: Tough one, prof. Don't forget we have to deal not just with your Institute, but the entire field of Cultural Affairs and Roman Catholi – Education.

EBENWALD: We did hope, Excellency, that since you were one of us, you'd show particular support for the field of medical education, so badly neglected under the previous Minister.

FLINT: (*To WINKLER.*) Bull's-eye! Achilles' heel! (*To EBENWALD.*) Keep this to yourself or they'll use it in the House, but sometimes I'm homesick for the sickroom. When you achieve something there, it gets noticed. Politicians only get recognition when they're six feet under.

The SECRETARY enters with another card.

WINKLER: Professor Tugendvetter.

FLINT: I'll leave him to you, Winkler. After you, professor.

FLINT and EBENWALD exit. TUGENDVETTER enters.

TUGENDVETTER: Privy counsellor. I won't keep you long. Just wondering how things are progressing in my little affair?

WINKLER: You're well on your way, professor.

TUGENDVETTER: Personally I don't care about awards for distinguished service, privy counsellor. But, *women,* you know...

WINKLER: No, professor.

TUGENDVETTER: Bachelor, eh? Anyway, mine's just dotty about the title of Privy Counsellor. If it were at all possible that the appointment could take place before her birthday? First of June? Be handy to give her my title as a gift.

WINKLER: Saves buying a brooch.

TUGENDVETTER: Anything you could do to, as it were, prod things a little –

WINKLER: (*Bureaucratically.*) Regrettably the Ministry is unable at present to allow private relations to prod the conferment of titles, such prodding requiring the imprimatur of particular imperial provisos.

The SECRETARY enters with a card.

(*Surprised.*) Ah.

SECRETARY: He'd like to speak to His Excellency in person.

WINKLER: Yes. Of course he would. But I'd be delighted to receive him in my office first.

The SECRETARY exits.

TUGENDVETTER: I'll go.

WINKLER: Don't. It's a mutual friend.

BERNHARDI enters. TUGENDVETTER is surprised.

BERNHARDI: You have company, privy counsellor.

TUGENDVETTER: Bernhardi!

WINKLER: (*Shaking his hand very warmly.*) I'm very happy to see you again, professor.

BERNHARDI: So am I, very happy.

TUGENDVETTER: Greetings, Bernhardi.

He holds out his hand. BERNHARDI takes it, coolly.

BERNHARDI: His Excellency?

WINKLER: Won't be a moment. Please, sit.

TUGENDVETTER: You...you look absolutely...super. I... Well, d'you know, it totally slipped my mind when you were due to be –

WINKLER: Congratulations on your ovation this morning.

TUGENDVETTER: Ova –?

BERNHARDI: You have your ears to the ground. 'Ovation' is pushing it.

WINKLER: Really? – I've even heard talk of a pageant in your honour. And the Chairman of the Society of Free-thinkers of Brigittenau has composed an anthem!

TUGENDVETTER: Two months...it can just fly-by, can't it?

BERNHARDI: Especially on a chain-gang.

TUGENDVETTER: On a...? Oh. You're absolutely glowing, really you are. Couldn't have looked better if he'd spent the summer on the Riviera. Super.

WINKLER: If *you'd* like to perpetrate a little 'religious agitation,' professor, I'm sure we could arrange you a cheap holiday somewhere custodial? Separate arrangements for your titled wife, of course.

TUGENDVETTER: (*Laughing.*) Oh, yes, very funny.

BERNHARDI: Actually, I was treated pretty well. Some angel had her eye on me: the guilty conscience of the men who threw me in there.

TUGENDVETTER: And I'm delighted to find this opportunity to say I was always on your side.

BERNHARDI: How unfortunate for you that it was lost for so long. I *am* relieved you located it.

FLINT and EBENWALD enter. They both compose themselves quickly at the sight of BERNHARDI.

FLINT: Bernhardi!

EBENWALD: Hello, professor.

BERNHARDI: Ebenwald. Here on Institute business?

EBENWALD: Yes.

FLINT: The subsidy…

BERNHARDI: I knew everything would be in safe hands – while I was away.

EBENWALD: Thank you for that, professor. Kind of you.

FLINT: You're here because –?

BERNHARDI: I won't keep you long, Flint.

WINKLER: Gentlemen?

He exits with EBENWALD and TUGENDVETTER.

FLINT: (*Quickly resolved.*) Good opportunity, old man, to wish you hearty congratulations on your release. Unhappily, my official role meant it was impossible to, you know, let you know, appropriately, how shocked and embarrassed I was at the verdict. Anyway, done and dusted – so if there's anything you want, fire away.

BERNHARDI: How kind, Flint. I *am* here to ask a favour. It's about Archduke Konstantin – he's very ill.

FLINT: Ill…? The Archduke? I hadn't heard.

BERNHARDI: He's called for me.

FLINT: What's stopping you?

BERNHARDI: I don't want to trouble the law again.

FLINT: Why should you?

BERNHARDI: You know perfectly well it would be quackery if I attended the Archduke. As I let myself agitate religiously, and get convicted for it, I forfeited my right to practice. You've shown before, old friend, that you have some leverage with the Minister of Justice, so if you could lever him in my name again, then the Archduke won't have to wait.

FLINT: Got it. You're here to laugh at me.

BERNHARDI: Why so? I don't want to be thrown in the clink, as good as they were to me last time, so if you'd be so kind – (*He hands him his appeal.*)

FLINT: Done. Take full responsibility. See no reason why you can't treat the Archduke within the hour. No legal comeback, you have my word. Good enough?

BERNHARDI: In this case keeping it shouldn't be *too* hard.

FLINT: Bernhardi!

BERNHARDI: Excellency?

FLINT: Archduke my bloody foot! (*He composes himself immediately.*) You accuse me of breaking my word, is that it?

BERNHARDI: Yes, Flint.

FLINT: My response: I did not. The only word I gave was that I'd stand up for you. And I couldn't have done that better than by aiming for clarity – i.e. a trial. Anyway, this is ridiculous: a private denunciation had already been made against you, and the inquiry couldn't be stopped. None of that was anything to do with me. It's about time you understood that there are higher things in public life than 'keeping your word' as you define it, Bernhardi. They're to keep your eye on the target, to not let your work get pulled from under your rug. Toes. I realised that as I was about to take your side in Parliament that day and felt the white-hot umbrage of the men around me.

BERNHARDI: So you simply altered your position.

FLINT: My friend, I could have tripped into an abysmal pit with you – and in doing so committed a crime against my calling and country – or I could sell you down the river since you were in any case sold. In a flash I chose the latter, so I could build new scientific institutes, modernise the faculties, improve public health, reform our spiritual life. I don't think these things have been paid for *too* dearly by eight weeks clapped in irons – especially as you weren't even clapped in irons. Because I hope you don't think I admire your martyrdom. If you'd borne all this bother in the name of something great – of an idea, of your religion, of your fatherland – then I'd have some real respect for you. But let me tell you as an old friend, I see in your entire behaviour nothing more than a tragicomedy of bloody-mindedness – and furthermore I doubt very much if you'd have stuck to your rock so comprehensively were it still the Austrian thing to tie people to stakes and set them on fire.

BERNHARDI stares at him for a while, then begins to clap.

FLINT: How dare you.

BERNHARDI: Just in case you missed it.

FLINT: Honestly, some half-baked joke?

BERNHARDI: Two friends in private. And I could never match your eloquence.

FLINT: Hmn. Well. Don't think the Ministry doesn't know what you're planning. Why on earth are you here? This pathetic Archduke ruse –

BERNHARDI: Obviously, Flint, I came to hear an explanation of your behaviour towards me. For 'His Excellency and the Convict' – pretty good title for the last chapter of a book, don't you think? Were a book worth bothering with.

FLINT: Oh, bother, *do.* It could double as your inaugural speech when you become a politician. Surely only a matter of hours before you get a Social Democrat mandate, they're handing them out like bon-bons this week.

BERNHARDI: Politics is your game, old friend.

FLINT: Politics?! Bugger politics. I took on this portfolio because I knew there was no one else in Austria who could do what needs to be done. I won't be hanging round long after I've put down the baton on the overture, that's for sure. I'm a doctor. That's the real me. I'm a teacher of medicine. I long to get back on the ward, to look out on a sea of student faces in a lecture hall. All this is just an interlude–

WINKLER enters.

WINKLER: Apologies, Excellency…but I've just received an urgent message from Mr Bermann, at the Ministry of Justice – and it concerns Professor Bernhardi.

BERNHARDI: Me?

WINKLER: The nurse, Ludmilla, the Crown witness in your case, has lodged an appeal accusing herself of lying in court.

BERNHARDI: She what – ?

FLINT: But –

WINKLER: Bermann will be here soon to make a detailed report to you.

FLINT: She's lodged it? It's being processed?

WINKLER: Yes. You'll demand a new trial of course, Professor Bernhardi?

BERNHARDI: A new trial – ? You are joking? Never.

FLINT: What? But –

BERNHARDI: Why? New light on an old hoax? – still a hoax. Anyone with sense knows I was innocent – and I can't get my two months back.

FLINT: Oh you do bang on about those two months! As if they matter a fig. We're talking about higher values here. You've no sense of justice, Bernhardi.

BERNHARDI: I'm gathering that.

FLINT: What else, Winkler?

WINKLER: The curious thing is that Ludmilla first *confessed* her false testimony. That is, in the confessional. Her confessor then asked her to make good her sin.

FLINT: Her priest?

WINKLER: Clearly he didn't have a clue who she was.

FLINT: That is a quite a statement, sir: what proof do you have of that?

BERNHARDI: I can't go to court again. I'll certify Ludmilla's an hysterical lunatic.

FLINT: How like you.

BERNHARDI: What have I got to gain from having the poor woman gaoled?

WINKLER: She might have company inside. Don't forget that other witness, Mr Hochroitzpointner. He'll be feeling the heat. In fact, fate is already bearing down on him.

BERNHARDI: Fate in the form of Kurt Pflugfelder?

WINKLER: Yes.

FLINT: You seem to know everything, Winkler.

WINKLER: It's in the job description, Excellency.

BERNHARDI: Kurt has better things to do than take up arms against a double-dealing medical student.

FLINT: (*Pacing.*) In the confessional! Well, won't *this* bamboozle certain individuals! It could turn out that Catholic customs may occasionally be extremely helpful to Jews.

BERNHARDI: I don't want helpful customs, I want peace!

WINKLER: I think this one's going to run, with or without you.

BERNHARDI: Then it'll be without me.

FLINT: I'd like to point out, Bernhardi, it isn't really down to what you want. It'd be rather quaint, wouldn't it, now that we're on the path of justice, if you were to go off the beaten track and start fraternising with layabouts and so forth in the woods, hacks and so on...

BERNHARDI: It's over.

FLINT: Fancy.

BERNHARDI: Done with.

FLINT: Hmn. But your pamphlet...or is it a book? I heard some tittle-tattle about a *book*, didn't I?

BERNHARDI: There's no book now – and if there's another trial, my statement from the first is on record – I've nothing to add. I don't need to be summoned.

FLINT: But you won't be able to stop *me* if I think I should appear in court. Even you'll understand, Bernhardi, my intention from the beginning of this entire affair was to aim for *clarity*. The first trial was of course a necessity – or how would we have arrived at the second? I foresee the bright light of transparency this time. Now we mustn't be rash. Hasty climbers have sudden falls. (*He taps at his breast pocket.*)

BERNHARDI: What's that?

FLINT: A letter, my friend. A certain old letter that might yet have its day in the coming clash. *Your* letter, explaining the ins and outs of the whole affair, the rock-bottom *truth*!

The SECRETARY enters.

SECRETARY: Mr Bermann, from the Ministry of Justice, Excellency, he'd like to see you in–

FLINT: Oh, goodie! (*To BERNHARDI.*) If you'd be kind enough to stay for a moment?

BERNHARDI: Archduke Konstantin –

FLINT: – has the constitution of several large animals. He's waited two long months for you, I don't think he's going to keel over in the next half hour. Keep him here, Winkler. We may need to put our heads together, plan the attack. Not a lot to ask, after everything, my old friend.

He exits after the SECRETARY.

BERNHARDI: I've got to get out of Vienna.

WINKLER: It's just beginning. And what about your patients?

BERNHARDI: What am I going to do?

WINKLER: Get used to it. Wear it with pride.

BERNHARDI: Pride? Privy counsellor, you've no idea how ridiculous I feel. That reception at the gaol, the letters, the editorial in The Chronicle, did you read it? I was hot with shame. All my plans…my book… pointless. Ridiculous. The problem isn't Austrian politics, or politics at all…it's much more general and philosophical than that…ethical things: responsibility, revelation, free-will. In the face of everything, I wasn't even sure I still had a score to settle with Flint this morning. But I was resolved to see him. So I rushed here to tell him – well, you can guess. The reckoning. And I stood in front of him…and nothing. No anger left. You should have heard him! I couldn't be cross with him. I almost wonder if I ever was.

WINKLER: He's always liked you, professor.

BERNHARDI: Now Ludmilla? –

WINKLER: Yes.

BERNHARDI: Another trial? –

WINKLER: I think so.

BERNHARDI: I've got to escape, privy counsellor. I've lost my self-respect, I have to find it. The clamour! People are discovering I was right – I can't stick around for that!

WINKLER: But, professor, being right doesn't mean being popular. The odd politician catches the mood of his party: popularity by convenience, perhaps. Anyway, it's a conceit of yours, that you were right.

BERNHARDI: What?

WINKLER: You heard.

BERNHARDI: You think – ? What do you think? That I should have let the priest–

WINKLER: Oh, no doubt about it! Because you're not a born reformer, are you?

BERNHARDI: How many more times –

WINKLER: You don't have what it takes to go to the bitter end for your beliefs. To risk your life for them. I don't either. That's why the decent thing for the likes of us is to simply not get into this kind of pickle in the first place.

BERNHARDI: But –

WINKLER: There's nothing to be gained from it. Sparing that pitiful girl a fright on her deathbed was like trying to solve poverty by giving a beggar a castle.

BERNHARDI: Privy counsellor, like everyone else, you're forgetting I never wanted to solve anything. I just did in one case – in one case – what I thought was right.

WINKLER: Yes, you see, that was your cock-up. If I decided to always do the right thing …actually, if I unintentionally began one morning after breakfast to do the right thing, and continued to do the right thing the rest of the day, I'd be banged up by sundown.

BERNHARDI: Privy counsellor. If you were in my position, you'd have done exactly as I did.

WINKLER: Maybe. But then like you I'd have been a bloody fool. If you'll pardon me, Professor Bernhardi.

Curtain.

APPENDIX

Alternative Ending to Act Four

At BERNHARDI's line "Come in, Oskar." on page 117 cut the rest of the act and replace with the following:

OSKAR: Some telegrams have arrived for you.

BERNHARDI takes them and opens the door to the dining-room, revealing the others. Some of them are smoking.

CYPRIAN: Ah, at last!

ADLER: We're already on to cigars!

CYPRIAN: A patient, so late?

BERNHARDI: Hard to answer. Look, telegrams! (*He opens one.*) How kind.

CYPRIAN: Anyone we know?

BERNHARDI: An ex-patient. 'With me all the way.' Poor devil, an ill man.

GOLDENTHAL: May I? Florian Ebeseder?

LÖWENSTEIN: Well I never – a Christian.

KURT: (*Touching his shoulder.*) It happens!

BERNHARDI: (*Opening another telegram.*) Oh, God – (*He gives CYPRIAN the telegram.*)

The doorbell rings. OSKAR exits.

ADLER: Read it out!

CYPRIAN: 'We'll always be at the side of the brave freedom-fighter in the war against the enemies of enlightenment. Dr Reiss, Walter König…'

BERNHARDI: Never heard of them.

GOLDENTHAL: Very welcome support. I expect more of it.

BERNHARDI: What can we do to stop it?

GOLDENTHAL: (*Laughing.*) To stop it!?

OSKAR enters.

BERNHARDI: Who is it now?

OSKAR: The Chairman of the Society of Free-thinkers of Brigittenau. And a journalist from *The Chronicle.*

BERNHARDI: I'm not at home.

GOLDENTHAL: Why ever not?

BERNHARDI: Because I'm already in the dungeon. I've been executed.

OSKAR: Father, the journalist wants to know if you intend to appeal…and why you summoned Minister Flint.

BERNHARDI: Tell him thank you, but no thank you.

GOLDENTHAL: As your lawyer, my advice is to see him. It's best to confront rumours head-on. (*To OSKAR.*) Tell him my client is very tired. Tell him that though we have no desire to impugn the integrity of the Viennese jurors, the…factious nature of a certain section of the press compromised the case and paved the way for judicial error. Regarding any appeal, tell him we're pausing to reflect on the best course of action.

BERNHARDI: Tell him nothing of the sort.

GOLDENTHAL: Bernhardi, *The Chronicle*'s men have access to Flint. And they're standing up to him. I'd characterise it as moderate, even liberal. When Flint has been, well, counter-progressive…reactionary…*The Chronicle* has objected. They could be very helpful to us.

BERNHARDI: I don't want anything to do with people who want to make a political affair out of my business. This is a personal matter.

LÖWENSTEIN: The personal is often political.

BERNHARDI: I'm not responsible for the coincidence. I don't belong to any party, and I don't want to be claimed by *The Chronicle*, or anyone else.

GOLDENTHAL: (*To OSKAR.*) Wait, Dr Bernhardi –

BERNHARDI: No. Anyone who stands up for me does so at his own risk. (*Lightly, with his characteristic ironic smile.*) Today I was convicted of agitating the Catholic religion, tomorrow I might be accused of agitating something else – and it could be a bedfellow of *The Chronicle*'s. Say no, Oskar. My final word.

OSKAR exits.

GOLDENTHAL: Whether you like it or not, we're in the middle of a political fight. We should welcome –

BERNHARDI: Dr Goldenthal, I welcome nothing, least of all war-cries. I won't be seduced into any kind of role – precisely because it *is* a role. As for our pause for reflection, consider it done with.

GOLDENTHAL: But –

BERNHARDI: I want to start my punishment. Tomorrow, if the room's ready.

GOLDENTHAL: Professor, I –

BERNHARDI: I'm a doctor. I haven't done what I'm on this earth to do for months. Meetings, interrogations, and for what? The whole thing was tawdry enough in court; the last thing I want is a political fight. No appeal: send me to gaol. Then I can get back to my job.

LÖWENSTEIN: But your revenge?

BERNHARDI: Who said anything about revenge?

LÖWENSTEIN: Flint, Ebenwald! You're not going to let them off the hook!

BERNHARDI: That won't be a revenge. That'll be a reckoning. And it will happen. But I shouldn't devote my life to a scrap. I'll do that at my leisure. Don't worry, they won't get anything for free.

OSKAR enters.

OSKAR: He won't go away.

BERNHARDI: Please, no one give him food.

GOLDENTHAL: I urge you, Bernhardi – it's a friendly paper.

BERNHARDI: Dr Goldenthal, I have to take my enemies how and where I find them. Luckily, I can choose my friends.

End of Act Four.